Knits

to Give

Knits
to *Give*

30 knitted gift ideas

Debbie Bliss

Photography by Penny Wincer

Quadrille
PUBLISHING

Contents

After working for many years as a hand-knit designer, I sometimes struggle to recapture the sheer joy of knitting that comes from creating a project with only self-imposed deadlines as opposed to commercial ones. However, every time I pick up my knitting needles to make something for a family member or friend, I instantly feel that connection with the recipient: what it is that makes them dear to me. This is combined with the hope and anticipation that they will be delighted with my homemade gift, as it has been considered with care and my time and effort has been pored into producing something unique, created just for them.

Each week I hold a very informal knitting group, when I meet up with friends at a local bar-restaurant. These weekly craft sessions came into being because I was meeting so many neigbouring young mothers, all of whom wanted to take up knitting in order to make things for their new babies. Each one of them was a complete novice knitter. Mia, the amazing stylist for this book, started off by making simple squares so she could practice different stitch patterns. Once she had perfected a variety of stitches, Mia sewed all the squares together to make a patchwork. She gave this finished knitted blanket to a mother-to-be friend at her baby shower. Her friend's overwhelming response to this one-off, hand-crafted present taught Mia – hitherto renowned for her skills as a shopper rather than as a maker – the joy of both making and giving. It also reminded me once again just how pleasureable gift-giving can be.

The projects in Knits to Give have been divided into chapters – For Her, For Him, For Baby, For Kids, For Home – and are a mix of accessories, simple garments, toys and homewares – a broad range that will hopefully provide a gift solution for even the most difficult to buy for. Many of the knits are simple and quick to make, because there are always those birthdays or special anniversaries that we are only reminded of shortly before they occur. Other projects are more time-consuming to make, but that will be cherished forever.

In an age of the 'life on the go', bouncing between family, friends and work commitments, the easy option is often to grab a little something and wrap it quickly before heading off to a get-together. But set aside some time, choose an appropriate pattern, pick a favourite colour yarn and discover how rewarding making something special for someone special in your life can be.

Debbie Bliss

Types of Yarn

The yarns I have chosen for the designs in this book range from my organic cotton to cashmerinos and pure wools, each with their own contribution to make to the designs. It may be that they give crisp stitch detail in a simple pattern, such as the moss stitch table mats worked in cotton, or provide softness and cosiness in a baby shawl.

Unless you are using up your stash to make the smaller items in this book, make the effort to buy the yarn stated in the pattern. Each of these designs has been created with a specific yarn in mind.

A different yarn may not produce the same quality of fabric or have the same wash and wear properties. From an aesthetic point of view, the clarity of a subtle stitch pattern may be lost if a project is knitted in an inferior yarn. However, there may be occasions when a knitter needs to substitute a yarn – if there is an allergy to wool, for example – and so the following is a guideline to making the most informed choices.

Always buy a yarn that is the same weight as that given in the pattern: replace a double knitting with a double knitting, for example, and check that the tension of both yarns is the same.

Where you are substituting a different fibre, be aware of the design. A cable pattern knitted in cotton when worked in wool will pull in because of the greater elasticity of the yarn and so the fabric will become narrower; this will alter the proportions of the garment.

Check the metreage of the yarn. Yarns that weigh the same may have different lengths in the ball or hank, so you may need to buy more or less yarn.

Descriptions of my yarns used in this book and a guide to their weights and types are given on page 12.

Debbie Bliss Angel:
* A lightweight mohair-blend yarn.
* 76% superkid mohair, 24% silk.
* Approximately 200m/25g ball.

Debbie Bliss Baby Cashmerino:
* A lightweight yarn between a 4ply and a DK.
* 55% merino wool, 33% microfibre, 12% cashmere.
* Approximately 125m/50g ball.

Debbie Bliss Bella:
* A double-knitting-weight yarn.
* 85% cotton, 10% silk, 5% cashmere.
* Approximately 95m/50g ball.

Debbie Bliss Cashmerino Aran:
* An aran-weight yarn.
* 55% merino wool, 33% microfibre, 12% cashmere.
* Approximately 90m/50g ball.

Debbie Bliss Cashmerino DK:
* A double-knitting-weight yarn.
* 55% merino wool, 33% microfibre, 12% cashmere.
* Approximately 110m/50g ball.

Debbie Bliss Cotton DK:
* A double-knitting-weight yarn.
* 100% cotton.
* Approximately 84m/50g ball.

Debbie Bliss Eco Baby:
* A lightweight yarn between a 4ply and a DK.
* 100% organic cotton.
* Approximately 125m/50g ball.

Debbie Bliss Rialto Aran:
* An aran-weight yarn.
* 100% extra fine merino wool.
* Approximately 80m/50g ball.

Debbie Bliss Rialto DK:
* A double-knitting-weight yarn.
* 100% extra fine merino wool.
* Approximately 105m/50g ball.

Debbie Bliss Rialto Chunky:
* A chunky-weight yarn.
* 100% merino wool.
* Approximately 60m/50g ball.

Debbie Bliss Riva:
* A chunky-weight yarn.
* 70% wool, 30% acrylic.
* Approximately 80m/50g ball.

buying yarn
The ball band on the yarn will carry all the essential information you need as to tension, needle size, weight and yardage. Importantly it will also have the dye lot. Yarns are dyed in batches or lots, which can vary considerably. As your retailer may not have the same dye lot later on, buy all your yarn for a project at the same time. If you know that sometimes you use more yarn than that quoted in the pattern, buy extra. If it is not possible to buy all the yarn you need with the same dye lot, use the different ones where it will not show as much, on a neck or border, as a change of dye lot across a main piece will most likely show.

It is also a good idea at the time of buying the yarn that you check the pattern and make sure that you already have the needles you will require. If not buy them now, as it will save a lot of frustration when you get home.

abbreviations
In a pattern book general abbreviations will usually be given at the front before the patterns begin, whilst those more specific to a particular design will be given at the start of the individual pattern. The abbreviations on the next page are the ones used throughout this book.

Standard Abbreviations

alt	alternate
beg	begin(ning)
cont	continue
dec	decrease(ing)
foll	following
inc	increase(ing)
k	knit
kfb	knit into front and back of next stitch
m1	make one stitch by picking up the loop lying between the stitch just worked and the next stitch and working into the back of it
p	purl
patt	pattern
psso	pass slipped stitch over
rem	remain(ing)
rep	repeat(ing)
skpo	slip 1, knit 1, pass slipped stitch over
sl	slip
ssk	[slip 1 knitwise] twice, insert tip of left-hand needle from left to right through fronts of slipped stitches and k2tog
st(s)	stitch(es)
st st	stocking stitch
tbl	through back loop
tog	together
yf	yarn forward
yo or **yon**	yarn over needle
yrn	yarn round needle

Giftwrapping Ideas

An exquisitely wrapped gift is a desirable object in itself, which only adds to the excitement of receiving a present. When you have taken so much care in hand knitting a present, don't lessen the impact by scrimping on the wrapping. With so many ready-made boxes and bags available, not to mention endless pretty ribbons, there really is no excuse not to create the perfect present.

A gift is a token of your love and esteem, so do take care to present it perfectly. There are so many stylish ways to wrap a present, but often simplicity is the best approach. I love the look and feel of plain brown parcel paper tied with raffia or string, then finished with a luggage label used as a gift tag. Recycling paper as giftwrapping can look good as well as being eco conscious; leftover scraps of decorative wallpaper, out-of-date Ordnance Survey maps and even the prettily pink Financial Times newspaper all make interesting giftwrap.

The foolproof method of giftwrapping is, of course, to opt for one of the many ready-made gift boxes and bags. These can be a neat solution, although not always the most economic. Tissue paper is a good cost-effective choice, but you do need to use two or three sheets together for coverage. I always try to keep packs of coloured tissue paper in the cupboard along with a selection of ribbons.

If your gift is a garment or larger item, make sure that the hand knit is neatly folded. Layer the project with tissue paper to prevent the knit from from creasing. I recommend using acid-free tissue paper as it will prevent any discolouration if the hand knit is stored in the paper for any length of time. Adding tissue paper is also a useful way of filling out a giftbox as well as providing an extra shot of colour.

If the gift I am giving uses any buttons as part the design, such as the Tea Cosy Wrap on page 132, I like to include one or two extra buttons in the package just in case any get lost. So don't forget to add a couple of spares to your shopping list when you are collecting the materials needed to make the project.

Finally, remember to add the laundry instructions inside your parcel. Either save the ball band from the yarn used and tuck it into the giftwrapping or copy out the care information onto a pretty gift tag or card which the recipient can keep safe.

For Her

Beaded Clutch Bag

This elegant evening bag takes just a single ball of Baby Cashmerino to make, plus some inexpensive glass beads for added sparkle. Each bead is first threaded onto the yarn and then worked into the knitted fabric, creating a sophisticated chevron design. Although it's a deceptively simple project to make, whoever receives this bag cannot fail to be impressed.

size
Approximately 12 x 16cm (4¾ x 6¼in)

materials
✷ 1 x 50g ball of Debbie Bliss Baby Cashmerino in bright pink
✷ Pair of 3.25mm (US 3) knitting needles
✷ Approximately 60g of small glass embroidery beads – silver lined clear glass beads, size SB07 colour 1 (www.creativebeadcraft.co.uk)
✷ One fine collapsible-eye beading needle – S126 (www.creativebeadcraft.co.uk)
✷ 50 x 20cm (20 x 8in) fabric for lining
✷ Iron-on fabric interlining

tension
25 sts and 34 rows to 10cm (4in) square over unbeaded st st using 3.25mm (US 3) needles.

abbreviations
PB (place bead) bring yarn to front of work between needles, slip next st purlwise, push bead close to work, take yarn to back of work between needles to work next st. Also see page 13.

notes

* Before casting on, you need to thread the beads onto the yarn. If your beading needle is made from very fine gauge wire with a long collapsible eye, you can thread the beads directly onto the yarn. If you have to use a fine needle with a small eye, you need to thread the needle with a length of sewing thread tied to form a loop, then thread the yarn through the loop, so the beads thread onto the sewing thread first, then onto the yarn.

* The beads need to have a centre hole, large enough for two thicknesses of yarn to pass through, or you will not be able to thread the beads. You may find a few beads that have a slightly smaller centre hole, this is due to a thicker than normal coating of silver and you will need to discard these, but you will have more than enough to complete the bag.

* When working the back of the bag, turn the chart upside down as you will be repeating the chart from the 52nd to the 1st row.

to make (worked in one piece)

Front flap

With 3.25mm (US 3) needles, cast on 45 sts.

1st row (right side) (1st chart row) K2, [PB, k1] to last st, k1.

2nd and all wrong side rows P all sts, making sure beads sit on the right side of work.

3rd row K1, [PB, k1] to end.

Continue to work from chart until all 52 rows have been worked.

Foldline row (right side) P to end.

Back

Work from chart from 52nd to 1st row (see Notes), so ending with a right side row.

Base

P 5 rows.

Front

Next row (right side) Work across 1st chart row.

Cont to work from chart from 2nd to 49th row, so ending with a right side row.

Cast off knitwise on wrong side.

lining

Iron interlining onto wrong side of lining fabric. Using the knitted piece as a template, cut a piece of fabric, adding 1.5cm (⅝in) all around for seams. Fold seam allowance onto wrong side and press. Handsew lining to wrong side of knitted piece.

to make up

Fold the piece along the base and sew bag front to bag back along the side edges, allowing front flap to fold onto right side.

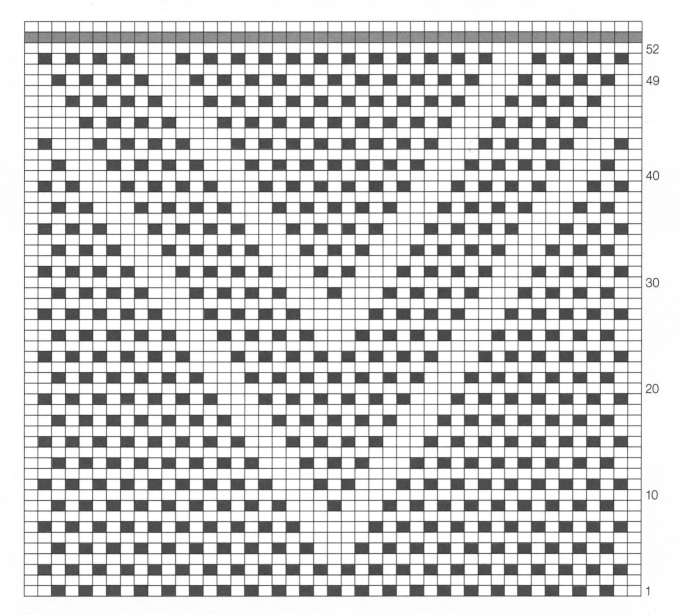

Key

□ K on right side rows and p on wrong side rows

■ PB place bead – see abbreviations on page 19

■ Foldline row – p on right side

Covered Bangles

If you are short on time but still want to give a handcrafted gift, these covered bangles are a satisfyingly quick knit. I have used three of my favourite texture stitches – moss stitch, blackberry stitch and cables with bobbles – to make a tonally harmonious trio. Included in the instructions are tips on how to adjust the sizing of the knitted pieces to fit your preferred bangles, big or small.

size

Knitted cover fits ready-made bangle. See page 27 for how to adjust size.

materials

Cable and bobble bangle

✶ 1 x 50g ball of Debbie Bliss Baby Cashmerino in camel

✶ Pair of 3.25mm (US 3) knitting needles

✶ One 3cm (1¼in) wide bangle with a circumference of 28cm (11in)

Moss stitch bangle

✶ 1 x 50g ball of Debbie Bliss Rialto Aran in ecru

✶ Pair of 4mm (US 6) knitting needles

✶ One 3cm (1¼in) wide bangle with a circumference of 28cm (11in)

Blackberry stitch bangle

✶ 1 x 50g ball of Debbie Bliss Rialto Aran in chocolate

✶ Pair of 4.50mm (US 7) knitting needles

✶ One 4cm (1½in) wide bangle with a circumference of 28cm (11in)

tension

It is not essential to work to an exact tension. See page 27 for how to adjust size.

abbreviations

MB [kfb] twice into next st, turn, p4, turn, k4, turn, [p2tog] twice, turn, k2tog.

T5R slip next 3 sts onto cable needle and hold at back of work, k2, then work [p1, k2] from cable needle.

C3BP slip next st onto cable needle and hold at back of work, k2, then p1 from cable needle.

C3FP slip next 2 sts onto cable needle and hold to front of work, p1, then k2 from cable needle.

Also see page 13.

note

* You can cover any size bangle, but if yours is wider or narrower than the ones here, you will need to adjust the number of stitches. The Blackberry Stitch and Moss Stitch bangles are worked to a length to fit the bangle, so any size can be worked, but with the Cable and Bobble bangle you may need to adjust the number of pattern repeats worked.

cable and bobble bangle

With 3.25mm (US 3) needles, cast on 19 sts.
1st row (right side) P7, T5R, p7.
2nd row K7, p2, k1, p2, k7.
3rd row P6, C3BP, p1, C3FP, p6.
4th row K6, p2, k3, p2, k6.
5th row P5, C3BP, p3, C3FP, p5.
6th row K5, p2, k5, p2, k5.
7th row P5, k2, p2, MB, p2, k2, p5.
8th row As 6th row.
9th row P5, C3FP, p3, C3BP, p5.
10th row As 4th row.
11th row P6, C3FP, p1, C3BP, p6.
12th row As 2nd row.
These 12 rows **form** the pattern and are repeated 6 times more.
Cast off.

to finish

Join cast on edge to cast off edge to make a circle.
Place around bangle.
Join row ends (sides) together, then slide around the bangle so the seam lies inside.

moss stitch bangle

With 4mm (US 6) needles, cast on 13 sts.
Moss st row K1, [p1, k1] to end.
Rep this row until strip fits around the outside circumference of bangle when slightly stretched.
Cast off.

to finish

Work as Cable and Bobble bangle.

blackberry stitch bangle

With 4.50mm (US 7) needles, cast on 14 sts.
1st row (right side) Purl.
2nd row K1, * [k1, p1, k1] into next st, p3tog; rep from * to last st, k1.
3rd row Purl.
4th row K1, * p3tog, [k1, p1, k1] into next st; rep from * to last st, k1.
These 4 rows **form** the pattern and are repeated until strip fits around the outside circumference of bangle.
Cast off.

to finish

Work as Cable and Bobble bangle.

Lacy Stole

This show-stopping stole would make such a special gift for a landmark birthday, anniversary or other significant event. In striking magenta pink, the stole makes a statement accessory suitable for a glamorous evening out, but if knitted up in a more neutral shade it could be worn more casually as a wrap over autumn weekends or curled up at home through winter nights.

size
Approximately 74 x 168cm (29 x 66in)

materials
* 10 x 25g balls of Debbie Bliss Angel in magenta
* Pair of 5mm (US 8) knitting needles

tension
18 sts and 23 rows to 10cm (4in) square over st st using 5mm (US 8) needles.

abbreviations
See page 13.

main piece

With 5mm (US 8) needles, cast on 132 sts.

K 3 rows.

Work in patt as follows:

1st row K3, [skpo, yf, k1, yf, k4, k2tog] to last 3 sts, k3.

2nd and every foll wrong side row K3, p to last 3 sts, k3.

3rd row K3, [skpo, k1, yf, k1, yf, k3, k2tog] to last 3 sts, k3.

5th row K3, [skpo, k2, yf, k1, yf, k2, k2tog] to last 3 sts, k3.

7th row K3, [skpo, k3, yf, k1, yf, k1, k2tog] to last 3 sts, k3.

9th row K3, [skpo, k4, yf, k1, yf, k2tog] to last 3 sts, k3.

11th row K3, p to last 3 sts, k3.

12th row K to end.

These 12 rows **form** the pattern and are repeated.

Cont in patt until stole measures approximately 167cm (65½in) from cast on edge, ending with a 9th row.

K 3 rows.

Cast off.

border

With 5mm (US 8) needles, cast on 10 sts.

K 1 row.

Work in patt as follows:

1st row K1, k2tog, yf, k3, [yf, k2tog] twice.

2nd row Yrn, k1, yf, k2tog, yf, k7. *12 sts.*

3rd row K1, k2tog, yf, k5, [yf, k2tog] twice.

4th row Yrn, k1, yf, k2tog, yf, k9. *14 sts.*

5th row K1, k2tog, yf, k7, [yf, k2tog] twice.

6th row Yrn, k1, yf, k2tog, yf, k11. *16 sts.*

7th row K1, k2tog, yf, k9, [yf, k2tog] twice.

8th row Yrn, k2tog, [yf, k2tog], twice, k10.

9th row K1, k2tog, yf, k6, [k2tog, yf] twice, k3tog. *14 sts.*

10th row Yrn, k2tog, [yf, k2tog], twice, k8.

11th row K1, k2tog, yf, k4, [k2tog, yf] twice, k3tog. *12 sts.*

12th row Yrn, k2tog, [yf, k2tog], twice, k6.

13th row K1, k2tog, yf, k2, [k2tog, yf] twice, k3tog. *10 sts.*

14th row Yrn, k2tog, [yf, k2tog], twice, k4.

These 14 rows **form** the pattern and are repeated.

Cont in patt until border fits along one side of stole, ending with a 14th row.

P 1 row.

Cast off.

to make up

Join straight edge of edging to one side of stole.

Pill Box Hat

Diamonds may be considered a girl's best friend, but to my mind pearls make an equally desirable gift. This screen siren-inspired pill box hat is liberally peppered with pearl beads, which contrast strikingly against the pillar box red yarn. Using a milliner's sinamay pill box base to provide the structure, the hat is knitted in stocking stitch with simple increases for the crown shaping.

size
To fit the pill box hat base (circumference approximately 51cm/20in)

materials
* 1 x 50g ball of Debbie Bliss Baby Cashmerino in red
* Pair of 3mm (US 2–3) knitting needles
* One 3mm (US 2–3) circular knitting needle
* 20cm (8in) diameter piece of lining fabric
* One sinamay pill box base SAC22 (www.millinerwarehouse.co.uk)
* 60cm (23½in) of 40mm (1½in) wide grosgrain ribbon
* One pack of 100 pearl beads – P10–1 100 (www.creativebeadcraft.co.uk)
* Approximately 40cm (15¾in) of hat elastic

tension
27 sts and 36 rows to 10cm (4in) square over st st using 3mm (US 2–3) needles.

abbreviations
See page 13.

to make

With 3mm (US 2–3) needles, cast on 6 sts.

1st row (right side) K1, [kfb] to last st, k1. *10 sts.*

2nd and every wrong side row P to end.

3rd row [Kfb] to last st, k1. *19 sts.*

5th row [K1, kfb] to last st, k1. *28 sts.*

7th row [K2, kfb] to last st, k1. *37 sts.*

9th row [K3, kfb] to last st, k1. *46 sts.*

Change to 3mm (US 2–3) circular needle.

Cont to inc 9 sts in this way on every right side row, working one more st before each inc as set until there are 145 sts, ending with the last inc row.

Beg with a p row, work straight in st st for a further 8cm (3¼in), ending with a p row. Cast off.

to finish

Join seam.

Place the circle of lining fabric inside the hat base and tack around the edge.

Place the knitted piece over the outside of the hat base and tack stitch to hold in place – the last row of shaping should match the top edge of the hat base. Fold the knitted piece inside the hat base and stitch in place, through the lining fabric and onto the base.

Using waxed thread (it is less likely to break than sewing thread), sew the pearl beads randomly over the outside of the hat.

Attach the hat elastic to the hat, securing in place.

Stitch one edge of the ribbon around the inside of the hat, folding the end under to neaten, and covering the knitted piece.

Cabled Arm Warmers

Fingerless mittens worked in chunky pure merino yarn are both a practical and sumptuous present. The generous rib cuff is designed to bridge the usual gap between coat sleeve and glove, while the open ends leave fingers free to garden or even to knit. The simple yet effective 'staghorn' cable that runs the length of the mittens is a good place to start for newcomers to cable knitting.

measurements
To fit average adult hands

materials
✳ 2 x 50g balls of Debbie Bliss Rialto Chunky in camel
✳ Pair of 6.50mm (US 10½) knitting needles
✳ Cable needle

tension
15 sts and 21 rows to 10cm (4in) square over st st using 6.50mm (US 10½) needles.

abbreviations
C4B slip next 2 sts onto cable needle, hold at back of work, k2, then k2 from cable needle.
C4F slip next 2 sts onto cable needle, hold to front of work, k2, then k2 from cable needle.
Also see page 13.

to make (make two, both alike)

With 6.50mm (US 10½) needles, cast on 38 sts.

1st row (right side) P2, [k2, p2, k2, p3] to end.

2nd row [K3, p2, k2, p2] to last 2 sts, k2.

These 2 rows **form** the rib and are repeated.

Work a further 3 rows in rib.

Inc row [K3, p2, m1, k2, m1, p2] to last 2 sts, k2. *46 sts.*

Cont in patt as follows:

1st row (right side) P2, [k8, p3] to end.

2nd row [K3, p8] to last 2 sts, k2.

3rd row P2, [C4B, C4F, p3] to end.

4th row [K3, p8] to last 2 sts, k2.

These 4 rows **form** the cable pattern and are repeated.

Patt a further 6 rows.

Dec row (right side) P2, [C4B, C4F, p2tog, p1] to end. *42 sts.*

Work a further 5 rows in patt as now set.

Dec row P2, [k8, p2tog] to end. *38 sts.*

Work a further 3 rows in patt as now set.

Thumb shaping

Next row Patt 19, m1, p1, m1, patt 18.

Work 1 row.

Next row Patt 19, m1, p3, m1, patt 18.

Work 1 row.

Next row Patt 19, m1, p5, m1, patt 18.

Work 1 row.

Next row Patt 19, m1, p7, m1, patt 18.

Work 1 row.

Next row Patt 19, m1, p9, m1, patt 18. *48 sts.*

Work 1 row.

Divide for thumb

Next row Patt 30, turn, cast on 3 sts.

Next row K14, turn.

Next row K2, [p2, k2] 3 times.

Next row P2, [k2, p2] 3 times.

Next row K2, [p2, k2] 3 times.

Cast off in rib.

Join seam.

With right side facing, join yarn to base of thumb, pick up and k one st, patt to end. *38 sts.*

Work 9 rows in patt.

Cast off in patt.

Join seam.

Ribbon-Tied Belt

This elegant cabled knitted strip is finished with the finest grosgrain ribbon tied in a bow to create a gorgeous belt. The ribbon ties make the belt fully adjustable, while the extra row of crochet along each edge helps the belt to sit neatly around the waist. Experiment with different colourways; use either coordinating or clashing ribbons.

size
Approximately 66cm (26in) long (excluding ribbon)

materials
* 1 x 50g ball of Debbie Bliss Bella in silver
* Pair of 3.75mm (US 5) knitting needles
* 3.25mm (US D/3) crochet hook
* 1m (1yd) of 15mm (⅝in) wide ribbon

tension
22 sts and 30 rows to 10cm (4in) square over st st using 3.75mm (US 5) needles.

note
If you are working a longer belt, you will need one more 50g ball of Bella.

abbreviations
C4B slip next 2 sts onto cable needle and hold at back of work, k2, then k2 from cable needle.

C4F slip next 2 sts onto cable needle and hold to front of work, k2, then k2 from cable needle.

C4BP slip next 2 sts onto cable needle and hold at back of work, k2, then p2 from cable needle.

C4FP slip next 2 sts onto cable needle and hold to front of work, p2, then k2 from cable needle.

Cr6L slip next 2 sts onto cable needle and hold to front of work, p2, k2, then k2 from cable needle.

Cr6R slip next 4 sts onto cable needle and hold at back of work, k2, then p4 from cable needle.

dc/sc double crochet in UK and single crochet in US.

Also see page 13.

to make

With 3.75mm (US 5) needles, cast on 20 sts.

1st row (right side) P1, k2, p2, k2, p6, k2, p2, k2, p1.

2nd row K1, p2, k2, p2, k6, p2, k2, p2, k1.

3rd to 12th rows Rep 1st and 2nd rows 5 times more.

13th row P1, k2, p2, Cr6L, C4BP, p2, k2, p1.

14th, 16th, 18th, 20th, 22nd and 24th rows (wrong side) K1, p2, k4, p6, k4, p2, k1.

15th, 19th and 23rd rows P1, k2, p4, k2, C4B, p4, k2, p1.

17th and 21st rows P1, k2, p4, C4F, k2, p4, k2, p1.

25th row P1, k2, p2, Cr6R, C4FP, p2, k2, p1.

26th row K1, p2, k2, p2, k6, p2, k2, p2, k1.

These 26 rows **form** the pattern and are repeated 7 times more, then work 1st to 11th rows once more.

Cast off in patt.

edging

With 3.25mm (US D/3) crochet hook and working from the wrong side, work 1dc (1sc) into every alternate st and row-end around the edges of the knitted strip. Fasten off.

to finish

Cut the ribbon into two pieces and folding 2cm (¾in) at one end of each piece, sew this end in place to the centre 6-st section at each end of the knitted strip.

For Him

Rice Stitch Scarf

Textural rice stitch – so called because the little bumps look like grains of rice – makes a fine alternative to moss stitch, but it is just as simple to knit. Rice stitch is the perfect choice for a scarf as, unlike stocking stitch, the side edges lay flat rather than roll inwards. Adapt the accent yarns that tip the scarf ends to suit the recipient; they could even reflect his favourite team colours.

size
Approximately 15 x 152cm (6 x 60in)

materials
* 3 x 50g balls of Debbie Bliss Rialto Aran in dark grey (A) and a small amount in each of fuchsia (B) and rust (C)
* Pair of 5mm (US 8) knitting needles

tension
22 sts and 24 rows to 10cm (4in) square over patt using 5mm (US 8) needles.

abbreviations
See page 13.

to make

With 5mm (US 8) needles and B, cast on 33 sts.

1st row (wrong side) P1, [k1tbl, p1] to end.

2nd row Knit.

These 2 rows **form** the pattern and are repeated.

Work a further 4 rows in patt.

Change to A and cont in patt until scarf measures 150cm (59in) from cast on edge, ending with a wrong side row.

Change to C and patt 6 rows.

Cast off in patt.

Fingerless Gloves

Whether he is out gardening, dog walking or goal keeping, the man in your life is sure to put to good use these practical fingerless gloves. Needing just a single ball of each colour yarn, this is an economic project to give as a gift. At one end the long ribbed cuffs keep wrists cosy, while at the other end the two-row stripes are echoed in the playful alternating of maroon and green fingers.

size
To fit medium hands

materials
* 1 x 50g ball each of Debbie Bliss Rialto DK in green (M) and maroon (C)
* Pair each of 3.25mm (US 3) and 3.75mm (US 5) knitting needles

tension
23 sts and 31 rows to 10cm (4in) square over st st using 3.75mm (US 5) needles.

abbreviations
See page 13.

right glove

** With 3.25mm (US 3) needles and C, cast 48 sts.

Rib row [K1, p1] to end.

Rib 1 more row.

Change to M.

Rib a further 32 rows.

Change to 3.75mm (US 5) needles and beg with a k row, work in st st.

Cont in stripes of 2 rows C and 2 rows M.

Work 6 rows. **

Thumb shaping

Next row K25, m1, k1, m1, k22.

Work 3 rows.

Next row K25, m1, k3, m1, k22.

Work 3 rows.

Next row K25, m1, k5, m1, k22.

Work 3 rows.

Next row K25, m1, k7, m1, k22.

Work 3 rows.

Next row K25, m1, k9, m1, k22. *58 sts.*

Work 3 rows, ending with 2 rows C.

Divide for thumb

Next row K37 in M, turn, cast on 3 sts.

Next row P16 in M.

Work 12 rows in st st in M only.

Cast off.

With right side facing and M, pick up and k3 sts from base of thumb, k to end. *48 sts.*

Work 13 rows in stripe sequence, so ending 2 rows M.

*** First finger

Next row K30 in C, turn and cast on 2 sts.

Next row P15 in C, turn, cast on 2 sts.

Cont in C only and work 10 rows in st st.

Cast off.

Join seam.

Second finger

With right side facing and C, pick up and k2 sts from base of first finger, k6, turn, cast on 2 sts.

Next row P15, turn, cast on 2 sts.

Change to M and work 12 rows st st.

Cast off.

Join seam.

Third finger

With right side facing and C, pick up and k2 sts from base of second finger, k6, turn, cast on 2 sts.

Next row P15, turn, cast on 2 sts.

Cont in C only and work 10 rows in st st.

Cast off.

Join seam.

Fourth finger

With right side facing and C, pick up and k2 sts from base of third finger, k6, turn.

Next row P15.

Change to M and work 6 rows st st.

Cast off.

Join seam.

left glove

Work as given for Right Glove from ** to **.

Thumb shaping

Next row K22, m1, k1, m1, k25.

Work 3 rows.

Next row K22, m1, k3, m1, k25.

Work 3 rows.

Next row K22, m1, k5, m1, k25.

Work 3 rows.

Next row K22, m1, k7, m1, k to end.

Work 3 rows.

Next row K22, m1, k9, m1, k to end. *58 sts.*

Work 3 rows, so ending 2 rows C.

Divide for thumb

Next row K34 in M, turn cast on 3 sts.

Next row P16 in M.

Cont in M only and work 12 rows st st.

Cast off.

With right side facing and M, pick up and k3 sts from base of thumb, k to end. *48 sts.*

Work 13 rows in stripe sequence, so ending 2 rows M.

Complete as for Right Glove from *** to end.

Walking Socks

Everyone deserves a touch of luxury in their life. These aran socks ensure happy feet, even when they are digging over the allotment or hiking across hills. The perfect pair of long socks to slip into walking boots or wellingtons, this design incorporates contrast colour heels and toes, plus a striped rib top. You only need a small amount of each, so use up any oddments for these accent colours.

size
To fit men's shoe size UK 9–10

materials
* 4 x 50g balls of Debbie Bliss Cashmerino Aran in plum (M) and 1 x 50g ball in each of gold (A), royal (B) and tangerine (C)
* Set of four 4.50mm (US 7) double-pointed knitting needles

tension
20 sts and 26 rows to 10cm (4in) square over st st using 4.50mm (US 7) needles.

abbreviations
See page 13.

to make

With 4.50mm (US 7) needles and A, cast on 64 sts.
Arrange these sts on 3 needles and cont in rounds.

Rib round [K2, p2] to end.

This round **forms** the rib and is repeated.

Work 1 more round.

Cont in rib in stripes of 2 rows each of [B, C, M and A] twice, B, C, then cont in M only until work measures 45cm (17¾in) from cast on edge.

Dec round [K2, p2tog] to end. *48 sts.*

Break yarn.

Divide sts onto 3 needles as follows: slip first 12 sts onto first needle, next 12 sts onto second needle, next 12 sts onto 3rd needle, then slip last 12 sts onto other end of first needle.

Shape heel

With right side facing, join A to 24 sts on first needle and work in rows on these 24 sts only.

Beg with a k row, work 13 rows in st st.

Shape heel

** **Next row** Sl 1, p to end.

Next row Sl 1, k13, skpo, k1, turn.

Next row Sl 1, p5, p2tog, p1, turn.

Next row Sl 1, k6, skpo, k1, turn.

Next row Sl 1, p7, p2tog, p1, turn.

Next row Sl 1, k8, skpo, k1, turn.

Next row Sl 1, p9, p2tog, p1, turn.

Next row Sl 1, k10, skpo, k1, turn.

Next row Sl 1, p11, p2tog, p1, turn.

Next row Sl 1, k12, skpo, turn.

Next row Sl 1, p12, p2tog, turn. *14 sts.*

Break off yarn.

Foot shaping

With right side facing and M, k14, pick up and k11 sts along side of back heel, k1, place a marker, k22 sts from needles, place a marker, k1, pick up and k11 sts along other side of back heel. *60 sts.*

Arrange these sts evenly on 3 needles and cont in rounds as follows:

1st round K to within 3 sts of marker k2tog, k1, slip marker, k to next marker, slip marker, k1, skpo, k to end.

2nd round K to end.

Rep the last 2 rounds 5 times more. *48 sts.*

Slipping markers on every round, work straight until sock measures 21cm (8¼in) from back of heel.

Change to B.

Shape toe

1st round K to within 3 sts of marker k2tog, k1, slip marker, k1, skpo, k to within 3 sts of next marker, k2tog, k1, slip marker, k1, skpo, k to end.

2nd round K to end.

Rep the last 2 rounds until 24 sts rem.

Slip first 6 sts onto one needle, next 12 sts onto a second needle, then slip rem 6 sts onto other end of first needle.

Transfer the two groups of sts onto safety pins, fold sock inside out, then transfer the sts back onto two needles and cast off one st from each needle together.

Make the second sock in exactly the same way.

iPad Cover

Tweed and leather are a classic combination, fit for every discerning gentleman. This cover for an original iPad or other tablet device is made from robust cotton knitted into a hardwearing tweed stitch fabric secured with fine leather ties. The pinstripe lining adds a splash of colour: you could always recycle a favourite shirt to personalise the present.

size
Approximately 66cm (26in) long (excluding ribbon) to closely fit an original iPad

materials
＊ 1 x 50g ball of Debbie Bliss Bella in chocolate
＊ Pair of 5mm (US 8) knitting needles
＊ 27 x 54cm (10¾ x 21¼in) piece of fine cotton fabric for lining
＊ 1m (1yd) of 15mm (⅝in) wide leather strip or ribbon

tension
23 sts and 38 rows to 10cm (4in) square over tweed st using 5mm (US 8) needles.

abbreviations
ytb take yarn to back of work between sts.
ytf bring yarn to front of work between sts.
Sl1p slip 1 st purlwise.
Also see page 13.

To make

With 5mm (US 8) needles, cast on 59 sts.

1st row (wrong side) K1, [ytf, sl1p, ytb, k1] to end.

2nd row (right side) P2, [ytb, sl1p, ytf, p1] to last st, p1.

These 2 rows **form** the tweed st patt and are repeated throughout.

Work in patt until piece measures 19cm (7½in), ending with a wrong side row.

Place a marker at each end of last row.

Cont in patt and cast on 2 sts at beg of next 2 rows. *63 sts.*

Cont in patt until piece measures 48cm (19in) from original cast on edge,
ending with a right side row.

Cast off knitwise.

To make up

Sew approximately 2cm (¾in) of one end of the leather or ribbon strip to the wrong
side of the knitted piece, placing it centrally behind the cast off edge. Fold 1cm (½in)
all around the edge of the fabric lining onto the wrong side and press in place. Slip
stitch the fabric to the wrong side of the knitted piece, placing it centrally, so the 2 sts
at each side that were cast on for the gusset remain unlined. Fold the piece across the
width where the 2 sts are cast on at each side. Sew the cast on sts at each side to the
row ends below the fold, so forming a small gusset, then continue to join the row ends
down to the cast on edge.

Moss Stitch Tie

I just love the combination of cherry red yarn and my all-time favourite moss stitch to make this tie. I've made it long enough to be tied into an old-fashioned windsor knot, however, if you want to make a smaller tie for a youngster, simply knit a shorter strip. Why not present the tie in a gift box along with step-by-step illustrations on how to tie a knot correctly, which can be easily found online?

size
142cm (56in) long

materials
* 2 x 50g balls of Debbie Bliss Baby Cashmerino in red
* Pair each of 2.75mm (US 2) and 3.25mm (US 3) knitting needles
* 38cm (15in) of 2.5cm (1in) wide grosgrain ribbon

tension
28 sts and 48 rows to 10cm (4in) square over moss st using 3.25mm (US 3) needles.

abbreviations
See page 13.

To make
With 3.25mm (US 3) needles, cast on 13 sts.
Moss st row K1, [p1, k1] to end.
This row **forms** moss st and is repeated throughout.
Cont in moss st until strip measures 66cm (26in) from cast on edge.
Place markers at each end of last row.
Change to 2.75mm (US 2) needles.
Cont in moss st for a further 4 rows.
Dec row K1, [p1, k1] twice, p3tog, [k1, p1] twice, k1. *11 sts.*
Cont in moss st until strip measures 103cm (40½in) from cast on edge.
Place markers at each end of last row.
Change to 3.25mm (US 3) needles.
Cont in moss st until strip measures 142cm (56in) from cast on edge.
Cast off in moss st.

To finish
Neaten ribbon by folding 1.5cm (5/8in) at each end onto wrong side and stitch folds
in place. Stitch ribbon to wrong side of tie centrally between markers. If preferred, you
can also fold the edges of the cast on and cast off edges onto the wrong side to make
points at each end of the tie. Position the ribbon backed section of the tie around the
neck to lie under the collar, before tying.

Houndstooth Dog Jacket

As a dedicated dog lover, I simply couldn't resist including a gift for Man's Best Friend! Whether pedigree or pooch, no dog could fail to look dapper in this houndstooth check. The instructions given here are suited to a medium-sized breed, such as my own Beagle, Monty, but the jacket is held in place using elastic and hook and loop fastener for both adaptability and ease.

size
To fit a medium-sized dog

materials
✳ 2 x 50g balls of Debbie Bliss Rialto Aran in black (A) and 1 x 50g ball in red (B)
✳ Pair of 4.50mm (US 7) knitting needles
✳ 1.5cm (⅝in) piece of 2cm (¾in) wide sew-on hook and loop fastener (Velcro®)
✳ Approximately 65cm (25½in) of 2cm (¾in) wide elastic

tension
23 sts and 24 rows to 10cm (4in) square over patterned st st using 4.50mm (US 7) needles.

abbreviations
See page 13.

note
Written instructions are given for the overall shape of the jacket, but the chart is used to place the 4-st, 4-row houndstooth pattern. When working from the chart, weave the yarn not in use across the wrong side of the work.

houndstooth pattern

Worked over 4 sts.

1st row (right side) K1A, k1B, k2A.

2nd row P3B, p1A.

3rd row K3B, k1A.

4th row P1A, p1B, p2A.

These 4 rows **form** the check pattern and are repeated.

to make

With 4.50mm (US 7) needles and A, cast on 70 sts.
Beg with a k row, work in st st and placing the pattern
as shown on the chart on page 71, shape as follows:
Work 4 rows.

Next row (right side) Kfb, k to last 2 sts, kfb, k1.

P 1 row.

Rep the last 2 rows 3 times more. *78 sts.*

Work 8 rows straight.

Next row (right side) Skpo, k to last 2 sts, k2tog.

Work 3 rows.

Rep the last 4 rows 5 times more. *66 sts.*

Work 20 rows straight.

Next row (right side) Kfb, k to last 2 sts, kfb, k1.

Work 3 rows.

Rep these 4 rows 3 times more. *74 sts.*

Shape neck

Next row (right side) K26, turn and cont on these sts
only, leave rem sts on a spare needle.

Cast off 2 sts at beg (neck edge) of next row and
3 foll wrong side rows. *18 sts.*

K 1 row.

Next row (wrong side) P2tog, p to end.

Work 6 rows.

Next row Skpo, k to last 2 sts, k2tog.

P 1 row.

Rep the last 2 rows twice more.

Next row Skpo, k to end.

P 1 row.

Rep the last 2 rows once more. Cast off rem 9 sts.
With right side facing, rejoin A to sts on spare needle,
cast off 22 sts, patt to end. P 1 row.

Cast off 2 sts at beg (neck edge) of next row and
3 foll right side rows. *18 sts.*

P 1 row.

Next row (right side) Skpo, k to end.

Work 5 rows.

Next row Skpo, k to last 2 sts, k2tog.

P 1 row.

Rep the last 2 rows twice more.

Next row Skpo, k to end.

P 1 row.

Rep the last 2 rows once more. Cast off rem 9 sts.
Press on wrong side.

edging

With 4.50mm (US 7) needles and A, cast on 5 sts.

Moss st row K1, [p1, k1] twice.

This row is repeated throughout.

Work in moss st until strip fits around the edge of the jacket,
allowing extra to accommodate the corners and neck edge.
Do not cast off, leave the sts on a holder and do not cut
the yarn, this will enable you to either add or subtract
more rows if necessary.

to finish

Working through the edge st of the edging, sew in place
around the jacket, easing around the corners and neck
edge. Cast off the 5 sts and join the ends.

Sew one piece of loop and hook fastener to the neck
edging – the loop on the right side of the right front neck
and the hook on the wrong side of the left front neck, to
fasten around the dog's neck.

Put the jacket onto the dog and fasten at the neck, mark
the position for the elastic, then remove the jacket. Fold
1cm (½in) at each end of the elastic onto the wrong side
and sew the folds in place. Sew one end of the elastic to
the wrong side of the edging at the right hand side of the
jacket. Sew the remaining piece of loop and hook fastener
to the elastic and the edging – the hook to the elastic and
the loop to the edging on the left hand side of the jacket;
the elastic goes under the dog to hold the jacket in place.

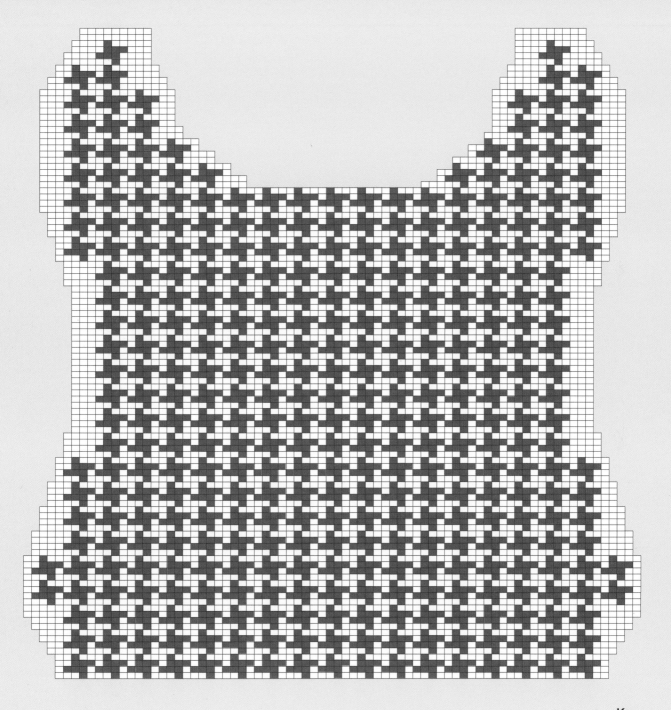

Key

☐ A

■ B

For Baby

Baby Shawl

Pretty enough for a special Christening gift, yet cosy enough for everyday use, this baby's shawl is the perfect way to welcome a precious newborn into the world. The relief of the embossed leaf stitch design works just as well in other pale pastel shades or even classic white. Guaranteed to melt any new parent's heart, this shawl will become an instant family heirloom.

size
Approximately 70 x 85cm (27½in x 33½in)

materials
✳ 10 x 50g balls of Debbie Bliss Baby Cashmerino in pale pink
✳ One 3.25mm (US 3) circular knitting needle

tension
25 sts and 34 rows to 10cm (4in) square over st st using 3.25mm (US 3) needles.

abbreviations
See page 13.

to make

With 3.25mm (US 3) needles, cast on 182 sts.

P 1 row.

Work in patt as follows:

1st row P2, [k9, k3tog, yf, k1, yrn, p2] to end.

2nd and every foll wrong side row K2, [p13, k2] to end.

3rd row P2, [k7, k3tog, k1, yf, k1, yf, k1, p2] to end.

5th row P2, [k5, k3tog, k2, yf, k1, yf, k2, p2] to end.

7th row P2, [k3, k3tog, k3, yf, k1, yf, k3, p2] to end.

9th row P2, [yon, k1, yf, sl 1, k2tog, psso, k9, p2] to end.

11th row P2, [k1, yf, k1, yf, k1, sl 1, k2tog, psso, k7, p2] to end.

13th row P2, [k2, yf, k1, yf, k2, sl 1, k2tog, psso, k5, p2] to end.

15th row P2, [k3, yf, k1, yf, k3, sl 1, k2tog, psso, k3, p2] to end.

16th row K2, [p13, k2] to end.

These 16 rows **form** the pattern and are repeated.

Cont in patt until work measures 85cm (33½in) from cast on edge, ending with a 15th patt row.

Next row P to end.

Cast off.

Bunny Bootees

Who could resist this cute pair of bunnies, with their long floppy
ears and twitchy noses. Perhaps best of all, these bootees can be
made using just one ball of Cashmerino DK yarn, plus oddments
for the pompon tail and embroidery details. They will keep a young
baby's toes cosy, before they become a toddler and start
hopping about themselves.

size
To fit age 3–6 months

materials
* 1 x 50g ball of Debbie Bliss
Cashmerino DK in duck egg blue (A) and
ecru (B) and oddments of chocolate yarn
for embroidery
* Pair of 3.25mm (US 3) knitting needles

tension
25 sts and 34 rows to 10cm (4in) square
over st st using 3.25mm (US 3) needles.

abbreviations
See page 13.

main part (make 2)

With 3.25mm (US 3) needles and A, cast on 36 sts.
K 5 rows.
Beg with a k row, work 7 rows in st st.
K 2 rows.
Rib row [K1, p1] to end.
Rep the rib row 9 times more and inc 3 sts evenly across last row. *39 sts.*
Beg with a k row, work 4 rows in st st.

Shape instep

Next row K26, turn.
Next row P13, turn.
Work 13 rows in st st on these 13 sts only.
Next row P3, [p2tog, p3] twice.
Break off yarn.
With right side facing, rejoin yarn at base of instep, pick up and k8 sts along side edge of instep, k11 sts of instep, pick up and k8 sts along other side of instep, k rem 13 sts. *53 sts.*
Beg with a p row, work 14 rows in st st.
Next row [P next st tog with corresponding st 7 rows below] to end.

Shape sole

Next row Sl first 21 sts onto right hand needle, rejoin yarn and k10, k2tog, turn.
Next row Sl 1, k9, k2tog tbl, turn.
Next row Sl 1, k9, k2tog, turn.
Rep last 2 rows 8 times more, then work first of the 2 rows again.
Next row Sl 1, k3, sl 1, k2tog, psso, k3, k2tog, turn.
Next row Sl 1, k7, k2tog tbl, turn.
Next row Sl 1, k7, k2tog, turn.
Rep last 2 rows once more, then work first of the 2 rows again.

Next row Sl 1, k2, sl 1, k2tog, psso, k2, k2tog, turn.
Next row Sl 1, k5, k2tog tbl, turn.
Next row Sl 1, k5, k2tog, turn.
Rep last 2 rows 3 times more.
Next row Sl 1, k2, k2tog, k1, k2tog tbl.
Place rem sts at each side of sole on one needle, with the needle point in same direction as the needle with sole sts. With right sides together and taking one st from each needle each time, cast off rem sts together.

outer ears (make 4)

With 3.25mm (US 3) needles and A, cast on 7 sts.
Beg with a k row, work 12 rows in st st.
Next row K1, [k2tog, k1] twice.
Work 3 rows.
Next row K2tog, k1, k2tog.
Next row Work 3tog.
Fasten off.

inner ears (make 4)

With 3.25mm (US 3) needles and B, cast on 5 sts.
Beg with a k row, work 12 rows in st st.
Next row K2tog, k1, k2tog.
Work 3 rows.
Next row Work 3tog.
Fasten off.

to make up

Join back seam of main part of each bootee, reversing seam on cuff. Turn back cuff. Sew inner ears to outer ears. Fold in half at cast on edge and stitch together first 4 rows of outer layers. Sew ears in place and embroider eyes and nose with chocolate yarn.

Moss Stitch Dungarees

These smart dungarees are deceptively easy to make but are sure to be a hugely appreciated gift. Knitted in my favourite moss stitch, with rib cuffs and bib, only minimal shaping is required. If you don't want to tackle a buttonhole, simply add a large press stud instead. Either way, the practical shoulder fastenings make it easy to slip the dungarees on and off a wriggling child.

measurements

To fit ages

0–3	3–6	6–9	9–12	mths

Finished measurements

Chest

50	54	59	64	cm
19¾	21¼	23¼	25½	in

Length to shoulder (adjustable)

42	45	48	51	cm
16½	17¾	19	20	in

Inside leg length

10	11	12	13	cm
4	4¼	4¾	5	in

materials

* 4(5:5:6) x 50g balls of Debbie Bliss Baby Cashmerino in faded blue
* Pair each of 2.75mm (US 2) and 3.25mm (US 3) knitting needles
* 2 buttons

tension

26 sts and 44 rows to 10cm (4in) square over moss st using 3.25mm (US 3) needles.

abbreviations

y2rn yarn round needle twice to make 2 sts. Also see page 13.

back

First leg

With 2.75mm (US 2) needles, cast on 32(34:36:38) sts.

Rib row [K1, p1] to end.

Rep the last row 7 times more.

Change to 3.25mm (US 3) needles.

1st moss st row (right side) [K1, p1] to end.

2nd moss st row [P1, k1] to end.

These 2 rows **form** the moss st.

Inc row (right side) Inc in first st, moss st to end.

Work 3 rows.

Rep the last 4 rows 6(7:8:9) times more and the inc row again. *40(43:46:49) sts.*

Cont straight until leg measures 10(11:12:13)cm/ 4(4¼:4¾:5)in, ending with a wrong side row.

Shape crotch

Next row (right side) Cast off 4 sts, patt to end. *36(39:42:45) sts.*

Patt 1 row.

Leave these sts on a holder.

Second leg

With 2.75mm (US 2) needles, cast on 32(34:36:38) sts.

Rib row [K1, p1] to end.

Rep the last row 7 times more.

Change to 3.25mm (US 3) needles.

1st moss st row (right side) [P1, k1] to end.

2nd moss st row [K1, p1] to end.

These 2 rows **form** the moss st.

Inc row (right side) Patt to last 2 sts, inc in next st, patt last st.

Work 3 rows.

Rep the last 4 rows 6(7:8:9) times more and the inc row again. *40(43:46:49) sts.*

Cont straight until leg measures 10(11:12:13)cm/ 4(4¼:4¾:5)in, ending with a right side row.

Shape crotch

Next row (wrong side) Cast off 4 sts, patt to end. *36(39:42:45) sts.*

Patt 1 row.

Next row Patt 35(38:41:44), work last st tog with first st of left leg, patt 35(38:41:44). *71(77:83:89) sts.*

Next row Patt to end.

Next row Patt 34(37:40:43), work 3 tog, patt 34(37:40:43).

Patt 15 rows.

Next row Patt 33(36:39:42), work 3 tog, patt 33(36:39:42).

Patt 15 rows.

Next row Patt 32(35:38:41), work 3 tog, patt 32(35:38:41). *65(71:77:83) sts.*

Cont straight until back measures 27(29:31:33)cm/ 10¾(11½:12¼:13)in from cast on edges, ending with a wrong side row.

Next row P1, [k1, p1] to end.

Next row K1, [p1, k1] to end.

Rep the last 2 rows 7 times more.

Shape armholes

Cast off 6(8:8:10) sts at beg of next 2 rows.
53(55:61:63) sts.

Next row K2, [p1, k1] to last 3 sts, p1, k2.

Next row K1, [p1, k1] to end. **

Rep the last 2 rows until armhole measures
8(9:10:11)cm/3¼(3½:4:4¼)in, ending with
a wrong side row.

Shape back neck

Next row K2, [p1, k1] 3(3:4:4) times, p1, k2, turn
and work on these sts only for first strap.

Next row K1, [p1, k1] to end.

Next row K2, [p1, k1] to last st, k1.

Cont in rib as set until strap measures 10cm (4in),
ending with a wrong side row.

Cast off in rib.

With right side facing, rejoin yarn to rem sts, cast off
centre 31(33:35:37) sts, with one st on needle after
cast off, [k1, p1] 4(4:5:5) times, k2.

Next row K1, [p1, k1] to end.

Next row K2, [p1, k1] to last st, k1.

Work on these sts in rib as set, until strap measures
10cm (4in), ending with a wrong side row.

Cast off in rib.

front

Work as given for Back to **.

Rep the last 2 rows until armhole measures 4(5:6:7)cm/
1½(2:2¼:2¾)in, ending with a wrong side row.

Shape front neck

Next row K2, [p1, k1] 3(3:4:4) times, p1, k2, turn
and work on these sts for first strap.

Next row K1, [p1, k1] to end.

These 2 rows **form** the rib.

1st buttonhole row Rib 3(3:4:4), work 2 tog, y2rn,
work 2 tog, rib to end.

2nd buttonhole row Rib to end, working twice into y2rn.

Work a further 8 rows.

Cast off in rib.

With right side facing, rejoin yarn to rem sts, cast off
centre 31(33:35:37) sts, with one st on needle after
cast-off, [k1, p1] 4(4:5:5) times, k2.

Next row K1, [p1, k1] to end.

1st buttonhole row Rib 4(4:5:5), work 2 tog, y2rn,
work 2 tog, rib to end.

2nd buttonhole row Rib to end, working twice into y2rn.

Work a further 8 rows.

Cast off in rib.

to make up

Join inner leg and side seams. Try the dungerees on the
baby and mark the position for the buttons on the back
straps. Sew on buttons to match markers.

Garter Stitch Jacket

Handmade gifts will always be treasured, whatever they are. The time invested in creating something unique is a reflection of the maker's feelings. Preparing for parenthood is an extra-special time and many mothers-to-be like to share this moment with their family and friends by throwing a baby shower. This elegant baby jacket, knitted all in one piece, couldn't be a more perfect present.

measurements

To fit ages

0–3	3–6	6–9	mths

Finished measurements

Chest

46	50	54	cm
18	19¾	21¼	in

Length to back neck

22	25	28	cm
8¾	10	11	in

Sleeve length

11.5	14	16.5	cm
4¼	5½	6½	in

materials

* 3(4:4) x 50g balls of Debbie Bliss Baby Cashmerino in pale grey (M)
* Pair of 3.25mm (US 3) knitting needles
* 3 buttons
* 1m (1yd) of narrow ribbon

tension

25 sts and 50 rows to 10cm (4in) square over garter st using 3.25mm (US 3) needles.

abbreviations

See page 13.

to make (worked in one piece)

Left front

With 3.25mm (US 3) needles, cast on 55(63:71) sts.

K 5 rows (for button band).

** Next 2 rows K29(35:41), turn, k to end.

Next 2 rows K40(47:54), turn, k to end.

Next 2 rows K51(59:67), turn, k to end.

K 2 rows across all 55(63:71) sts. **

Rep from ** to ** 8(9:10) times more.

Next row K29(35:41), turn and cont on these sts only, leave rem 26(28:30) sts on a holder for yoke.

K 5 rows.

Leave these 29(35:41) sts on a holder for back.

Left sleeve

With 3.25mm (US 3) needles, cast on 29(35:41) sts.

K 5 rows.

Working across 29(35:41) sts of sleeve and 26(28:30) sts of yoke; rep from ** to ** 7(8:9) times.

Next row K29(35:41), turn and cont on these sts only, leave 26(28:30) sts of yoke on a holder.

K 5 rows.

Cast off.

Back

Return to 29(35:41) sts of back on holder.

K 6 rows.

Working across 29(35:41) sts of back and 26(28:30) sts of yoke, rep from ** to ** 18(19:20) times.

Next row K29(35:41), turn and cont on these sts only, leave rem 26(28:30) sts of yoke on a holder.

K 5 rows.

Leave these 29(35:41) sts on a holder for right front.

Right sleeve

Work as given for Left Sleeve.

Right Front

Return to 29(35:41) sts of right front on holder.

Work 6 rows.

Working across 29(35:41) sts of right front and 26(28:30) sts of yoke, rep from ** to ** 9(10:11) times.

K 2 rows.

Buttonhole row K29(35:41), yf, k2tog, [k9(10:11), yf, k2tog] twice, k2.

K 2 rows.

Cast off.

to make up

Using a flat seam, join sleeve seams. Join underarm seam. Sew on buttons. Thread the ribbon around the yoke, level with the centre buttonhole.

Sun Hat

During the warmer months young skin needs protection from the sun, so this floppy-brimmed hat is the ideal accessory to pack when heading off on your family summer holiday. Made with Eco Baby, this breathable cotton knit will help to keep baby cool. All you need is a single ball of the main shade of yarn, but you can then use up leftover oddments for the contrast colour picot edging.

measurements

To fit ages

0–3	3–6	6–9	mths

materials

* 1 x 50g ball of Debbie Bliss Eco Baby in pale green (M) and small amounts in duck egg blue (A) and aqua (B)
* Pair each of 3.25mm (US 3) and 5mm (US 8) needles

tension

25 sts and 34 rows to 10cm (4in) square over st st using 3.25mm (US 3) needles.

abbreviations

See page 13.

main part

With 3.25mm (US 3) needles and M, cast on 92(101:110) sts.

Beg with a k row, work 24(26:28) rows in st st.

Shape crown

1st row [K8(9:10), k2tog] 9 times, k2. *83(92:101) sts.*

2nd row P to end.

3rd row [K7(8:9), k2tog] 9 times, k2.

4th row P to end.

5th row [K6(7:8), k2tog] 9 times, k2.

6th row P to end.

7th row [K5(6:7), k2tog] 9 times, k2.

8th row P to end.

9th row [K4(5:6), k2tog] 9 times, k2.

10th row P to end.

11th row [K3(4:5), k2tog] 9 times, k2.

12th row P to end.

13th row [K2(3:4), k2tog] 9 times, k2.

14th row P to end.

15th row [K1(2:3), k2tog] 9 times, k2. *20(29:38) sts.*

16th row P to end.

2nd and 3rd sizes only

17th row [K–(1:2), k2tog] 9 times, k2. *–(20:29) sts.*

18th row P to end.

3rd size only

19th row [K1, k2tog] 9 times, k2. *–(–:20) sts.*

20th row P to end.

All sizes

Next row [K2tog] 10 times.

Next row [P2tog] 5 times.

Leaving a long end, cut yarn, thread through rem sts, pull up and secure.

brim

With right side facing, 3.25mm (US 3) needles and M, pick up and k92(99:106) sts evenly along cast on edge of main part.

Beg with a p row, work in st st.

Work 1 row.

1st inc row (right side) K1, [m1, k6(7:8), m1, k7] 7 times. *106(113:120) sts.*

Work 2 rows.

2nd inc row [P8, m1, p7(8:9), m1] 7 times, p1. *120(127:134) sts.*

Work 2 rows.

3rd inc row K1, [m1, k8(9:10), m1, k9] 7 times. *134(141:148) sts.*

Work 2 rows.

4th inc row [P10, m1, p9(10:11), m1] 7 times, p1. *148(155:162) sts.*

K 2 rows.

Edging

Change to A and beg with a k row, work 4 rows in st st.

Change to 5mm (US 8) needles and B.

Picot row K1, [yf, k2tog] to end.

Change to 3.25mm (US 3) needles and work 4 rows.

Cast off with 5mm (US 8) needles.

to make up

Join seam. Fold edging along picot row and slip stitch cast off edge to the inside of the brim.

Zebra Toy

Inspired by the animals of the African savannahs, there is no mistaking this knitted zebra with his distinctive black and white stripes. With his luxurious mane and swishy tail, this handsome zebra is a welcome addition to any baby's toy shelf to sit alongside the more conventional teddy bears and dolls. You can even dress him up in a smart cotton apron trimmed with ricrac.

size
Approximate height 25cm (10in)

materials
* 1 x 50g ball of Debbie Bliss Rialto DK in each of black (A) and ecru (B)
* Pair of 3.25mm (US 3) knitting needles
* Washable toy stuffing (see Notes)
* 12 x 24cm/43/4 x 91/2in piece of fabric (optional)
* 1m (1yd) of ricrac braid (optional)

tension
25 sts and 56 rows to 10cm (4in) square over striped garter st using 3.25mm (US 3) needles.

abbreviations
s2togkpo slip next 2 sts tog, k1, then pass slipped sts over knit st.
Also see page 13.

notes
* All parts are worked using 3.25mm (US 3) needles.
* Worked in 2-row gt st stripes of A and B.
* Use a washable toy stuffing that is also non-flammable (flame retardant) and non toxic and adheres to UK and EU safety regulations (BS5852, BS1425, EN71, PT2)
* For the optional apron, follow the cutting guide below for the fabric, edge with the ricrac and use ricrac for straps and ties.

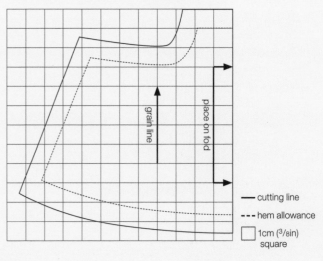

grain line

place on fold

— cutting line
--- hem allowance
☐ 1cm (3/8in) square

front legs (make 2)

Hoof

With A, cast on 4 sts.

Next row (right side) With A, [kfb] 3 times, k1. *7 sts.*

P 1 row A.

Next row With A, [k1, m1, k2, m1] twice, k1. *11 sts.*

Beg with a p row, work 2 rows st st in A.

Next row (wrong side) With A, p3, p2tog tbl, p1, p2tog, p3. *9 sts.*

Leg

K 2 rows B.

K 1 row A.

Next row (wrong side) With A, k3, [m1, k3] twice.

Beg with B and cont in garter st stripes of 2 rows B and 2 rows A, k 22 rows, so ending with a 2-row stripe in B. Leave sts on a holder.

body front (worked from base upwards)

With A, cast on 13 sts and k 1 row.

Next row (right side) With B, k6, m1, k1, m1, k6. *15 sts.*

K 1 row B.

K 2 rows A.

Next row With B, k7, m1, k1, m1, k7. *17 sts.*

K 1 row B.

K 2 rows A.

Beg with B, k a further 22 rows in 2-row stripes, so ending with a B stripe.

Leave sts on the needle.

body back

Work exactly as given for Body Front.

upper body

With right side facing and A, k across 17 sts of Body Back, k11 sts of Left Front Leg, k17 sts of Body Front, k11 sts of Right Front Leg. *56 sts.*

K 1 row A.

Next row With B, [ssk, k13, k2tog, ssk, k7, k2tog] twice. *48 sts.*

K 1 row B.

K 2 rows A.

Next row With B, [ssk, k3, ssk, k1, k2tog, k3, k2tog, ssk, k5, k2tog] twice. *36 sts.*

K 1 row B.

K 2 rows A.

Next row With B, [ssk, k1, ssk, k1, k2tog, k1, k2tog, ssk, k3, k2tog] twice. *24 sts.*

K 1 row B.

K 2 rows A.

Next row With B, [ssk, s2togkpo, k2tog, ssk, k1, k2tog] twice. *12 sts.*

K 1 row B.

K 2 rows A.

Cut yarn, thread through rem 12 sts, pull up and secure.

Join shaped edges of upper body, then continue to join side seam.

Join rem side seam and join front leg seams.

Stuff front legs and body, leaving cast on body edges open.

head

With A, cast on 5 sts.

Next row (right side) [Kfb] 4 times, k1. *9 sts.*

P 1 row.

Next row [K2, m1] twice, k1, [m1, k2] twice. *13 sts.*

P 1 row.

Now work in 2-row garter st stripes of B and A throughout as follows:

K 2 rows B.

Next row (right side) With A, k1, m1, k to last st, m1, k1. *15 sts.*

K 9 rows.

Next row K4, m1, k1, m1, k5, m1, k1, m1, k4. *19 sts.*

K 11 rows.

Next row K4, ssk, ssk, k3, k2tog, k2tog, k4. *15 sts.*

K 1 row.

Next row K3, ssk, ssk, k1, k2tog, k2tog, k3. *11 sts.*

K 1 row.

Next row K1, ssk, ssk, k1, k2tog, k2tog, k1. *7 sts.*

Next row (wrong side) Ssk, s2togkpo, k2tog. *3 sts.*

Cut yarn and thread through rem sts, pull up and secure. Join seam, leaving a small gap, stuff head lightly, close gap in seam.

Work a few sts in A on the head for the eyes, then work a central stitch in B on each eye.

ears (make 2)
With A, cast on 3 sts.

K 2 rows.

Next row S2togkpo.

Fasten off.

Sew ears in place to head.

back legs (make 2)
With A, cast on 8 sts and p 1 row.

Next row (right side) [Kfb] 7 times, k1. *15 sts.*

P 1 row.

Next row K1, m1, k4, [m1, k1] 6 times, k3, m1, k1. *23 sts.*

P 1 row.

Next row K9, k2tog, k1, ssk, k9. *21 sts.*

P 1 row.

Next row K8, k2tog, k1, ssk, k8. *19 sts.*

Next row P7, p2tog tbl, p1, p2tog, p7. *17 sts.*

Next row K7, s2togkpo, k7. *15 sts.*

P 1 row.

Next row K5, k2tog, k1, ssk, k5. *13 sts.*

P 1 row.

Beg with 2 rows in B, k 44 rows in 2-row garter st stripes of B and A throughout.

Cast off.

Join seam, leaving cast off edges open. Stuff lightly. With seams at the back, sew legs together side by side at the top edge.

to make up
Position joined back legs inside the open edge of the body and stitch in place all around, so closing all open edges. Sew head in place onto the body. Tie a piece of ribbon around the neck (optional).

For optional apron, see Notes on page 96.

tail
Make a plait with 6 strands of yarn, knot the end and cut the strands to finish the tail. Sew to the back of the body.

mane
Step 1
Thread a 8cm (3¼in) loop of yarn through the eye of the needle and insert the point of the needle from top to bottom through bar in the centre of a stitch.

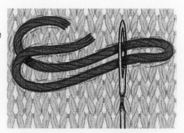

Step 2
Pull yarn loop through, then remove needle. Pass the 2 yarn ends through the loop.

Step 3
Place the needle under the double yarn above the loop and pull the yarn ends to tighten the loop onto the yarn.

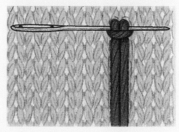

Repeat these steps working mane down the centre back head and part way down the centre back body, making sure the yarn is securely held in place so it can't be easily removed, you may need to add a couple of stitches in sewing thread to each tuft to make absolutely sure.

For Kids

Hairband With Bow

There really couldn't be a simpler or speedier project to make, yet this sweet hairband with bow is extremely effective. Have fun mixing and matching different colours – I just love this combination of coral pink yarn and apple green ribbon. As an alternative to a hairband, you could always attach a brooch back to the reverse of the bow so it can then be pinned on to either a jacket or a bag.

size
To fit a child of any age as ribbon length is adjustable

materials
* 1 x 50g ball of Debbie Bliss Eco Baby in coral
* Pair of 3mm (US 2–3) knitting needles
* 1m (1yd) of 1cm (½in) wide ribbon (or length to suit)

tension
It is not essential to work the bow to an exact tension.

abbreviations
See page 13.

bow

Main section

With 3mm (US 2–3) needles, cast on 12 sts.

Work in garter st (k every row) until strip measures approximately 16cm (6¼in).

Cast off.

Join cast on and cast off edges together.

Centre band

With 3mm (US 2–3) needles, cast on 6 sts.

Work in garter st (k every row) until strip measures approximately 7cm (2¾in).

Cast off.

Join cast on and cast off edges together.

to finish

Making sure the seam lies in the centre, pinch the middle of the main section, then slide the centre band into position with the seam at the back. Thread the ribbon through the centre band, behind the bow. Stitch the centre band in place to the main section. Tie around the head.

Ladybird Backpack

With its unmistakeable red and black spotty wings, this backpack is transformed into a ladybird bag – perfect for carrying school books, playtime toys or a packed lunch. When worn over the shoulders, the webbing straps become the ladybird's antennae. To carry on the spotty theme, I have lined the backpack with a printed cotton of black with red dots but any lining fabric will do.

size
28cm (11in) high and 23cm (9in) wide

materials
* 2 x 50g balls of Debbie Bliss Rialto Aran in black (A) and 1 x 50g ball in red (B)
* Pair each of 4.50mm (US 7) and 5mm (US 8) knitting needles
* 0.5m (½yd) of cotton fabric for lining
* 25cm (10in) zip fastener
* 23 x 8cm (9 x 3¼in) stiff card for base
* Two x 25mm (cat no: 64395) black plastic side release buckles with fixed bar (www.kleins.co.uk)
* Two x 20cm (8in) of 25mm wide black cotton webbing
* Two x 41cm (16in) of 38mm wide black cotton webbing

tension
18 sts and 24 rows to 10cm (4in) square over st st using 5mm (US 8) needles.

abbreviations
See page 13.

base
With 4.50mm (US 7) needles and A, cast on 68 sts.
K 1 row.
1st inc row (right side) K17, m1, k1, m1, k32, m1, k1, m1, k17.
K 1 row.
2nd inc row K17, m1, k3, m1, k32, m1, k3, m1, k17.
K 1 row.
3rd inc row K17, m1, k5, m1, k32, m1, k5, m1, k17.
K 1 row.
Cont to inc 4 sts in this way on 4 foll right side rows, working two more k sts between each pair of increase sts, until there are 96 sts, ending with the 7th increase row.
K 1 row.
Change to 5mm (US 8) needles.
Place chart on page 111 as follows:
Next row (right side) K27A, k across 42 sts of 1st row of chart, k27A.
Next row K2A, p25A, p across 42 sts of 2nd row of chart, p25A, k2A.

These 2 rows set the position of the chart in st st with 2-sts in garter st to each side.

Cont in this way until 48th chart row has been worked.

Next row (right side) With A, k22, ssk, k2tog, k1, k across 49th chart row, with A, k1, ssk, k2tog, k22. *92 sts.*

Next row With A, k2, p23, p across 50th chart row, with A, p23, k2.

Next row With A, k25, p across 51st chart row, with A, k25.

Next row With A, k2, p23, p across 52nd chart row, with A, p23, k2.

Next row With A, k21, ssk, k2tog, k across 53rd chart row, with A, ssk, k2tog, k21. *88 sts.*

Next row With A, k2, p21, p across 54th chart row, with A, p21, k2.

Next row With A, k20, ssk, k2tog, k across 40 sts of 55th chart row, with A, ssk, k2tog, k20. *84 sts.*

Next row With A, k2, p20, p across 40 sts of 56th chart row, with A, p20, k2.

Next row With A, k19, ssk, k2tog, k across 38 sts of 57th chart row, with A, ssk, k2tog, k19. *80 sts.*

Next row With A, k2, p19, p across 38 sts of 58th chart row, with A, p19, k2.

Next row With A, k18, ssk, k2tog, k across 36 sts of 59th chart row, with A, ssk, k2tog, k18. *76 sts.*

Next row With A, k2, p18, p across 36 sts of 60th chart row, with A, p18, k2.

Next row With A, k17, ssk, k2tog, k across 34 sts of 61st chart row, with A, ssk, k2tog, k17. *72 sts.*

Next row With A, k2, p17, p across 34 sts of 62nd chart row, with A, p17, k2.

Cont in A only and work as follows:

Divide for backs and front

Next row (right side) K16, ssk, turn and cont on these 17 sts for right back, leave rem sts on spare needle.

Next row P2tog tbl, p13, k2.

Next row K14, ssk.

Next row Slipping the first st, cast off 2, p to last 2 sts, k2.

Next row K to end.

Rep the last 2 rows once more.

Next row Slipping the first st, cast off 3, p to last 2 sts, k2.

Next row K to end.

Next row Slipping the first st, cast off 3, p to last 2 sts, k2.

Next row K to end.

Cast off rem 5 sts.

With right side facing, rejoin yarn to sts on spare needle, k2tog, k32, ssk, turn and cont on these 34 sts only for front, leave rem sts on the spare needle.

Next row P2tog tbl, p to last 2 sts, p2tog.

Next row K2tog, k to last 2 sts, ssk.

Slipping the first st, cast off 2 sts at beg of next 4 rows, then cast off 3 sts at beg of foll 4 rows.

Cast off rem 10 sts.

With right side facing, rejoin yarn to sts on spare needle, k2tog, k to end.

Next row K2, p13, p2tog.

Next row K2tog, k to end.

Next row K2, p to end.

Next row Slipping the first st, cast off 2, k to end.

Rep the last 2 rows once more.

Next row K2, p to end.

Next row Slipping the first st, cast off 3, k to end.

Rep the last 2 rows once more.

Cast off rem 5 sts.

to make up

Join row ends of base, then continue to join back opening for 1cm (½in). Join the cast on edge to complete the base.

Join the top 1cm (½in) of back opening. Handsew the zip in place behind the open edges of the back opening. Round off the corners of the cardboard to fit into the base of the bag.

Using the cardboard as a template cut a piece of lining fabric, adding 1.5cm (⅝in) around the edge. Cut another piece of lining fabric approximately 55 x 31cm (21¾ x 12¼in), fold in half to form a tube and taking 1.5cm (⅝in) seams, stitch each end of the seam, leaving the centre open for approximately 25cm (10in), to match the centre back opening of the bag. Fold the base lining in

half and mark the centre of one long side, then matching the seam of the fabric tube to the base marker, sew the base into the tube. Fold the lining in half with the seam centrally placed and sew across the top of the lining, rounding the corners.

Neaten both ends of each length of tape, then assemble the two pieces of narrower tape in the pronged end of the side release buckles. Sew the end of each tape to the right side of the bag just above the base edge. Sew one end of each of the wider tapes to the wrong side of the

bag back, either side of the centre back seam, angling the tape so the two pieces form a V shape. Folding the free end of each tape, assemble them into the other half of the side release buckles and stitch firmly in place. Sew the shaped edges of the top of the bag in place, so completing the bag shape and enclosing the tapes. Insert the cardboard base into the bag and if necessary, hold in place by working a few sts through the cardboard and the bag. Insert the lining into the bag and slipstitch the opening edge to the zipper tape.

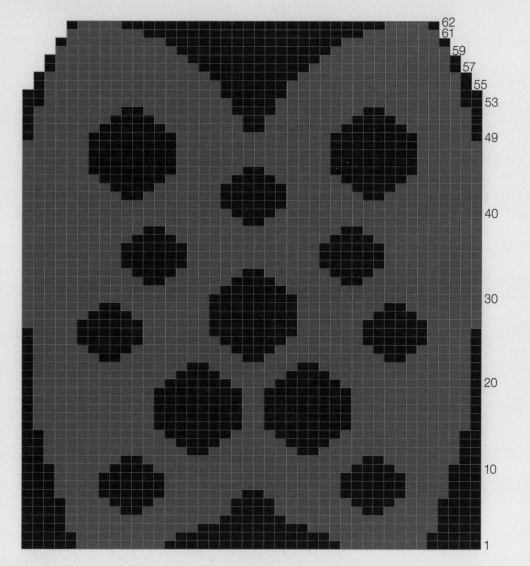

Key
■ A
■ B

Party Shrug

Every little girl looks pretty in pink. This slip-on shrug in a deep shade of coral mohair is the perfect partywear – teamed with a floaty dress it really does make an outfit fit for a princess. Made in an unconventional way, there is no back or front to be knitted for this shrug: the cast off edges of both sleeves are joined to make the centre back seam and the rib edging provides the collar.

measurements

To fit ages

2/3	3/4	4/5	years

Finished measurements

Across back

32	36	40	cm
12½	14¼	15¾	in

Length to centre back neck (incl border)

17	19	21	cm
6¾	7½	8¼	in

Sleeve length (with cuff turned back)

17	19	21	cm
6¾	7½	8¼	in

materials

* 2(2:3) x 25g balls of Debbie Bliss Angel in coral
* Pair each of 3.25mm (US 3), 4mm (US 6) and 4.50mm (US 7) knitting needles

tension

22 sts and 30 rows to 10cm (4in) square over st st using 4mm (US 6) needles.

abbreviations

See page 13.

right sleeve

With 4mm (US 6) needles, cast on 42(50:58) sts.

1st rib row K2, [p2, k2] to end.

2nd rib row P2, [k2, p2] to end.

Rep the last 2 rows 10 times more.

Place markers at each end of last row to indicate foldline. Change to 3.25mm (US 3) needles. Work 22 rows in rib. Change to 4mm (US 6) needles. Beg with a k row, work straight in st st until sleeve measures 17(19:21)cm/ 6¾(7½:8¼)in from foldline markers, ending with a p row. **

Shape top

Next row K3, skpo, k to end.

Place a second marker at beg of last row for start of Back.

Next row P to end.

Rep the last 2 rows 8 times more. *33(41:49) sts.*

Next row K3, skpo, k to end.

Next row P to last 5 sts, p2tog tbl, p3.

Rep the last 2 rows 5(7:9) times more. *21(25:29) sts.*

Work 18(20:22) rows straight. Cast off.

left sleeve

Work as given for Right Sleeve to **.

Shape top

Next row K to last 5 sts, k2tog, k3.

Place a marker at end of last row for start of Back.

Next row P to end.

Rep the last 2 rows 8 times more. *33(41:49) sts.*

Next row K to last 5 sts, k2tog, k3.

Next row P3, p2tog, p to end.

Rep the last 2 rows 5(7:9) times more. *21(25:29) sts.*

Work 18(20:22) rows straight. Cast off.

left front border and collar

With right side of left sleeve facing and 4mm (US 6) needles, pick up and k18(24:30) sts along straight back neck edge from end of cast off edge to start of raglan shaping, and 32(34:36) sts along raglan edge. *50(58:66) sts.*

1st row P2, [k2, p2] to end. This row **sets** the rib.

Next 2 rows Rib 10(14:18), turn, rib to end.

Next 2 rows Rib 14(18:22), turn, rib to end.

Next 2 rows Rib 18(22:26), turn, rib to end.

Next 2 rows Rib 22(26:30), turn, rib to end.

Cont in this way working 4 extra sts on every right side row until all sts have been worked, ending with a wrong side row. Work 2 rows in rib across all sts.

** Inc row (right side) K2, [p2, k1, m1, k1] to last 4 sts, p2, k2. *61(71:81)sts.*

Change to 4.50mm (US 7) needles.

Next row P2, [k2, p3] to last 4 sts, k2, p2.

Next row K2, [p2, k3] to last 4 sts, p2, k2.

The last 2 rows re-set the rib.

Rib a further 13 rows across all sts. Cast off loosely in rib. **

right front border and collar

With right side of right sleeve facing and 4mm (US 6) needles, pick up and k32(34:36) sts along raglan edge then 18(24:30) sts along straight back neck edge to end of cast off edge. *50(58:66) sts.*

Work in rib as set for Left Front Border and Collar.

Next 2 rows Rib 10(14:18), turn, rib to end.

Next 2 rows Rib 14(18:22), turn, rib to end.

Next 2 rows Rib 18(22:26), turn, rib to end.

Next 2 rows Rib 22(26:30), turn, rib to end.

Cont in this way working 4 extra sts on every right side row until all sts have been worked, ending with a right side row. Work 3 rows in rib across all sts.

Work as given for Left Front Border and Collar from ** to **.

lower back border

Join back seam (cast off sleeve edges) and collar seam, reversing last 10cm (4in) of collar seam.

With right side facing and 4mm (US 6) needles, pick up and k78(86:94) sts between both second markers.

1st row (wrong side) P2, [k2, p2] to end.

2nd row K2, [p2, k2] to end.

Rep the last 2 rows 8 times more and the first row again. Cast off in rib.

To finish, join sleeve seams and border seams.

Lion Cub Cravat

For the youngest member of your own pride, make this lion cub scarf with a huge amount of character. The knitting is divided to make a slot at one end, then the other end of the scarf is fed through this opening so that it will sit neatly and securely in place around the neck, even when your cub is running wild across the plains…or playground.

size
To fit a child of any age

materials
* 3 x 50g balls of Debbie Bliss Rialto DK in caramel (A) and 1 x 50g ball in each of orange (B), ecru (C) and black (D)
* Pair of 3.75mm (US 5) knitting needles

tension
24 sts and 33 rows to 10cm (4in) square over st st using 3.75mm (US 5) needles.

abbreviations
See page 13.

note
When working from chart, use separate small balls of yarn for each colour area and twist yarns at colour change to avoid holes.

head back

With 3.75mm (US 5) needles and B, cast on 9 sts.
Beg with a k row, work in st st throughout.
Work 2 rows.
3rd row Cast on 2 sts, k these sts, k to last st, m1, k1.
12 sts.
4th row Cast on 2 sts, p these sts, p to last st, m1, p1.
15 sts.
5th row K1, m1, k to last st, m1, k1. *17 sts.*
6th row P1, m1, p to last st, m1, p1. *19 sts.*
Work 2 rows.
9th row K1, m1, k to last st, m1, k1. *21 sts.*
Work 9 rows.
19th row K1, m1, k to last st, m1, k1. *23 sts.*
Work 3 rows.
23rd row K1, m1, k to last st, m1, k1. *25 sts.*
Work 1 row.
25th row K1, m1, k to last st, m1, k1. *27 sts.*
26th row P1, m1, p to last st, m1, p1. *29 sts.*
Work 2 rows.
29th row K1, m1, k to last st, m1, k1. *31 sts.*
Work 3 rows.
33rd row K1, m1, k to last st, m1, k1. *33 sts.*
Work 2 rows.
36th row P1, m1, p to last st, m1, p1. *35 sts.*
37th row K1, m1, k to last st, m1, k1. *37 sts.*
Work 1 row.
39th row K1, m1, k to last st, m1, k1. *39 sts.*
Work 4 rows.
44th row P2tog, p to last 2 sts, p2tog tbl. *37 sts.*
45th row Ssk, k to last 2 sts, k2tog. *35 sts.*
46th row P2tog, p7, turn, leave rem sts on the needle.
Next row Ssk, k4, k2tog.
Cast off rem 6 sts, slipping the first st and working last
2 sts tog.
With wrong side facing, rejoin yarn to rem 26 sts,
cast off 17 sts, p to last 2 sts, p2tog tbl. *8 sts.*
Next row Ssk, k4, k2tog.
Cast off rem 6 sts, slipping the first st and working last
2 sts tog.

face

With 3.75mm (US 5) needles and B, cast on 9 sts.
Beg with a k row, work in st st from chart throughout,
the shaping is worked in the same way as Head Back.

scarf

With 3.75mm (US 5) needles and A, cast on 60 sts.
1st row (right side) [K1, p1] to end.
2nd row [P1, k1] to end.
Rep these 2 rows once more.
Next row K1, p1, k27, p1, k1, p1, k27, p1.
Next row P1, k1, p27, k1, p1, k1, p27, k1.
These 2 rows **form** the pattern and are repeated.
Work a further 20 rows in patt.
Place markers at each end of last row.
Divide for opening
Next row (right side) K1, p1, k27, p1, turn and cont on
these 30 sts only, leave rem sts on a holder.
Next row P1, k1, p27, k1.
Patt a further 19 rows on these 30 sts, so ending
with a right side row.
Leave sts on a spare needle or holder.
With right side facing, rejoin yarn to 30 sts on first holder,
k1, p1, k27, p1.
Cont in patt on these 30 sts for a further 20 rows, so
ending with a right side row.
Joining row (wrong side) Patt across 30 sts on needle,
then patt across 30 sts on holder. *60 sts.*
Place markers at each end of last row.
Cont in patt until scarf measures 53cm (20¾in), ending
with a wrong side row.
Next row [K1, p1, k11, ssk, k2tog, k12, p1] twice. *56 sts.*
Patt 5 rows.
Next row [K1, p1, k10, ssk, k2tog, k11, p1] twice. *52 sts.*
Patt 5 rows.
Next row [K1, p1, k9, ssk, k2tog, k10, p1] twice. *48 sts.*
Patt 5 rows.
Cont to dec 4 sts in next row and every foll 6th row until
28 sts rem.
Cont straight in patt until scarf measures 71cm (28in)

from cast on edge, ending with a wrong side row.
Now work 3 rows in moss st across all sts.
Cast off in moss st.

to make up
Join Face and Head Back together around all edges.
Fold scarf in half lengthwise and join row ends, leaving a
gap in the seam between markers. Refold scarf so the
seam is central and join the cast on edge from fold to
fold. Match up central opening with gap in seam and join
around the edge. Position cast on edge of scarf behind
the head and sew in place, making sure, the opening
lies just above the head. Place around neck and thread
the narrower end of scarf from front to back through the
opening and pull through.

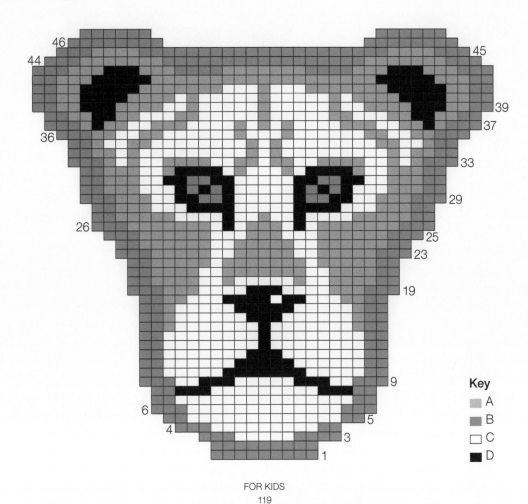

Key
■ A
■ B
□ C
■ D

Stripey Long Socks

Who says socks have to be a matching pair? As you can see, for a quirky touch, the striped colour bands are ever so slightly different on the right and left socks. They are knitted in the round on a set of four needles, but don't let that put you off. Once you get started, you'll soon get the hang of it. And the best part of all is that once you have finished knitting, there are no seams to sew.

size
To fit ages

4–6	6–8	years

materials
* 3 x 50g balls of Debbie Bliss Baby Cashmerino in grey (M) and 1 x 50g ball each of bright green (A), fuchsia (B), terracotta (C) and turquoise (D)
* Set of four 3.25mm (US 3) double-pointed knitting needles
* Two safety pins

tension
25 sts and 34 rows to 10cm (4in) square over st st using 3.25mm (US 3) needles.

abbreviations
See page 13.

stripe sequence for first sock

4 rows M, 6 rows A, 4 rows M, 14 rows B, 4 rows M,
4 rows C, 4 rows M, 10 rows D.

These 50 rows **form** the stripe patt and are repeated.

stripe sequence for second sock

4 rows M, 6 rows D, 4 rows M, 14 rows A, 4 rows M,
4 rows B, 4 rows M, 10 rows C.

These 50 rows **form** the stripe patt and are repeated.

to make

With 3.25mm (US 3) needles and M, cast on 80(88) sts.
Distribute sts evenly on 3 needles.

Work in correct stripe patt and rib as follows:

1st round [K1, p1] to end.

This round **forms** the rib and is repeated.

Work straight until sock measures 30(35)cm/12(14)in,
ending after 2 rows in M.

Cont in M only.

Next round [Skpo] to end. *40(44) sts.*

Cont in st st and work in rows not rounds.

Back heel shaping

1st row K9(10) turn.

2nd row Sl 1, p17(19), turn.

3rd row Sl 1, k17(19), turn.

Work on these 18(20) sts, arrange rem 22(24) sts on
two needles.

Rep the last 2 rows 8 times more, ending with a k row.

Shape heel

** Next row Sl 1, p to end.

Next row Sl 1, k9(11), skpo, k1, turn.

Next row Sl 1, p3(5), p2tog, p1, turn.

Next row Sl 1, k4(6), skpo, k1, turn.

Next row Sl 1, p5(7), p2tog, p1, turn.

Next row Sl 1, k6(8), skpo, k1, turn.

Next row Sl 1, p7(9), p2tog, p1, turn.

Next row Sl 1, k8(10), skpo, turn.

Next row Sl 1, p8(10), p2tog, turn. *10(12) sts.*

Foot shaping

With right side facing, k10(12), pick up and k12 sts along
side of back heel, k0(1), place a marker, k22(22) sts from
needles, place a marker, k0(1), pick up and k12 sts along
other side of back heel. *56(60) sts.*

Arrange these sts evenly on 3 needles and cont in
rounds as follows:

1st round K to within 3 sts of marker, k2tog, k1, slip
marker, k to next marker, slip marker, k1, skpo, k to end.

2nd round K to end.

Rep the last 2 rounds 7 times more. *40(44) sts.*

Slipping markers on every round, work straight until foot
measures 14(15)cm/5½(6)in from ** or until work fits
from back of heel to beg of toes.

Shape toe

1st round K to within 3 sts of marker k2tog, k1, slip
marker, k1, skpo, k to within 3 sts of next marker, k2tog,
k1, slip marker, k1, skpo, k to end.

2nd round K to end.

Rep the last 2 rounds until 20(20) sts rem.

Slip first 5 sts onto one needle, next 10 sts onto another
needle and rem and 5 sts onto end of first needle.

Transfer the two groups of sts onto safety pins, fold sock
inside out, then transfer the sts back onto two needles
and cast off one st from each needle together.

Cabled Slipover

An extremely useful cabled slipover with a wide neck, so it can be easily popped over young heads without any struggle. The stripe in the ribbed waistband and armhole cuffs is continued in the ribbed cowl collar. I have knitted it up in toning shades of mid and light blue, but this slipover would look equally great in white with a navy trim – perfect for a trip to the seaside or a game of junior cricket.

measurements

To fit ages

3–6	6–9	9–12	12–18	18–24	mths

Finished measurements

Chest

45	48	52	56	61	cm
17¾	19	20½	22	24	in

Length to shoulder

22	24	26	28	30	cm
8¾	9½	10¼	11	11¾	in

materials

* 2(2:3:3:3) x 50g balls of Debbie Bliss Baby Cashmerino in teal (M) and 1 x 50g ball in light blue (C)
* Pair each of 3mm (US 2–3) and 3.25mm (US 3) knitting needles
* One 3mm (US 2–3) circular knitting needle
* Cable needle

tension

32 sts and 34 rows to 10cm (4in) square over st st using 3.25mm (US 3) needles.

abbreviations

m1p make one (m1) purlwise.
C4F slip next 2 sts onto cable needle and hold to front of work, k2, then k2 from cable needle.
Also see page 13.

back

With 3mm (US 2–3) needles and C, cast on 58(66:74:82:90) sts.

1st row (right side) K2, [p2, k2] to end.

2nd row P2, [k2, p2] to end.

These 2 rows **form** the rib and are repeated.

Change to M.

Work a further 4 rows in rib.

Change to C.

Work a further 2 rows.

Change and cont in M only.

Work 1 row.

Inc row (wrong side) P2, k2(0:2:0:2), p2(0:2:0:2), [k2, m1p, p2, m1p, k2, p2] to last 4(0:4:0:4) sts, k2(0:2:0:2), p2(0:2:0:2). *70(82:90:102:110) sts.*

Change to 3.25mm (US 3) needles.

Cont in patt as follows:

1st row (right side) K2, p2(0:2:0:2), k2(0:2:0:2), [p2, k4, p2, k2] to last 4(0:4:0:4) sts, k2(0:2:0:2), p2(0:2:0:2).

2nd row P2, k2(0:2:0:2), p2(0:2:0:2), [k2, p4, k2, p2] to last 4(0:4:0:4) sts, p2(0:2:0:2), k2(0:2:0:2).

3rd row K2, p2(0:2:0:2), k2(0:2:0:2), [p2, C4F, p2, k2] to last 4(0:4:0:4) sts, p2(0:2:0:2), k2(0:2:0:2).

4th row As 2nd row.

5th row K2, p2(0:2:0:2), k2(0:2:0:2), [p2, k4, p2, k2] to last 4(0:4:0:4) sts, k2(0:2:0:2), p2(0:2:0:2).

6th row As 2nd row.

These 6 rows **form** the pattern and are repeated.

Cont in patt until back measures 12(13:14:17:19)cm/ 4¾(5:5½:6¾:7½)in from cast on edge, ending with a wrong side row.

Shape armholes

Cast off 3 sts at beg of next 2 rows. *64(76:84:96:104) sts. ***

Dec one st at each end of next row and 3(5:5:9:9) foll right side rows. *56(64:72:76:84) sts.*

Cont in patt until back measures 22(24:26:28:30)cm/ 8¾(9½:10¼:11:12)in from cast on edge, ending with a wrong side row.

Shape shoulders

Cast off 8(9:10:10:11) sts at beg of next 2 rows and 9(10:11:11:12) sts at beg of foll 2 rows.

Leave rem 22(26:30:34:38) sts on a holder.

front

Work as given for Back to **.

Shape front neck

Next row (right side) Work 2 sts tog, patt 27(33:37:43:47) sts, work 2 sts tog, turn and work on these 29(35:39:45:49) sts only for first side of front neck, leave rem 33(39:43:49:53) sts on a spare needle.

Next row Patt to end.

Next row Work 2 sts tog, patt to last 2 sts, k2tog.

Rep last 2 rows 2(4:4:8:8) times. *23(25:29:27:31) sts rem.*

Keeping armhole edge straight, dec one st at neck edge only on every foll right side row until 17(19:21:21:23) sts rem.

Cont straight until front measures same as Back to shoulder, ending at armhole edge.

Shape shoulder

Cast off 8(9:10:10:11) sts at beg of next row.

Work 1 row.

Cast off rem 9(10:11:11:12) sts.

With right side facing, rejoin yarn to sts on spare needle, cast off 1 st, skpo, cast off 1 st, patt to last 2 sts, work 2 sts tog.

Next row Patt to end.

Next row Skpo, patt to last 2 sts, work 2 sts tog.

Rep the last 2 rows 2(4:4:8:8) times. *23(25:29:27:31) sts rem.*

Keeping armhole edge straight, dec one st at neck edge on every foll right side row until 17(19:21:22:23) sts rem.

Cont straight until front measures same as Back to shoulder, ending at armhole edge.

Shape shoulder

Cast off 8(9:10:10:11) sts at beg of next row.

Work 1 row.

Cast off rem 9(10:11:11:12) sts.

collar

Join shoulder seams.

With right side facing, 3mm (US 2–3) circular needle and M, pick up and k36(38:40:44:46) sts evenly up right side of front neck, work p0(0:0:0:2), [k2tog], 0(0:0:2:2) times, k0(0:2:0:0), p0(2:2:2:2), k2, p2, [k2tog] twice, p2, k2, p2, [k2 tog] twice, p2, k2, p0(2:2:2:2), k0(0:2:0:0), [k2tog], 0(0:0:2:2) times, p0(0:0:0:2) across back neck sts, pick up and k36(38:40:44:46) sts evenly down left side of front neck. *90(98:106:114:122) sts.*

Work in rows not rounds.

1st, 3rd and 4th sizes only

1st row P2, [k2, p2] to end.

2nd and 5th sizes only

1st row K2, [p2, k2] to end.

All sizes

This row **sets** the rib patt.

Next 2 rows Rib to last 36(36:36:40:40) sts, turn.

Next 2 rows Rib to last 32(32:32:36:36) sts, turn.

Next 2 rows Rib to last 28(28:28:32:32) sts, turn.

Next 2 rows Rib to last 24(24:24:28:28) sts, turn.

Next 2 rows Rib to last 20(20:20:24:24) sts, turn.

4th and 5th sizes only

Next 2 rows Rib to last -(-:-:20:20) sts, turn.

All sizes

Next 2 rows Rib to last 16 sts, turn.

Change to C.

Next 2 rows Rib to last 12 sts, turn.

Change to M.

Next 2 rows Rib to last 8 sts, turn.

Next 2 rows Rib to last 4 sts, turn.

Rib to end.

Change to C.

Next row Rib to end.

With C, cast off in rib.

armbands

With right side facing, 3mm (US 2-3) needles and M, pick up and k78(82:86:94:98) sts evenly around armhole edge.

Change to C.

1st row K2, [p2, k2] to end.

2nd row P2, [k2, p2] to end.

These 2 rows **form** the rib pattern and are repeated.

Rib 4 rows M, and 1 row C.

With C, cast off in rib.

to make up

Lap left front collar over right and sew row ends to cast off sts at centre front.

Join side and armband seams.

For Home

Tea Cosy Wrap

There is nothing more comforting that a home-brewed pot of tea. But for me, tea has to be served piping hot and the only way to ensure this is with a tea cosy. This cabled aran cover neatly buttons around the teapot so it can be adjusted to fit most sizes; you could even adjust the proportions to suit a cafetiere if the intended recipient of your gift is a coffee lover rather than a tea drinker.

size
To fit a standard UK six-cup teapot

materials
* 1 x 50g ball of Debbie Bliss Cashmerino Aran in stone
* Pair each of 4mm (US 6) and 4.50mm (US 7) knitting needles
* 2 small buttons

tension
20 sts and 27 rows to 10cm (4in) square over st st using 4.50mm (US 7) needles.

abbreviations
C4B slip next 2 sts onto cable needle and hold at back of work, k2, then k2 from cable needle.

C4BP slip next 2 sts onto cable needle and hold at back of work, k2, then p2 from cable needle.

C4F slip next 2 sts onto cable needle and hold to front of work, k2, then k2 from cable needle.

C4FP slip next 2 sts onto cable needle and hold to front of work, p2, then k2 from cable needle.

Also see page 13.

pattern A (worked over 14 sts)
1st row (wrong side) K4, p6, k4.
2nd row P4, C4B, C4FP, p2.
3rd row K2, p2, k2, p4, k4.
4th row P4, k4, p2, C4FP.
5th row P2, k4, p4, k4.
6th row P4, C4B, p4, k2.
7th row As 6th row.
8th row P4, k4, p2, C4BP.
9th row As 4th row.
10th row P4, C4B, C4BP, p2.
11th row As 2nd row.
12th row P2, C4BP, C4F, p4.
13th row K4, p4, k2, p2, k2.
14th row C4BP, p2, k4, p4.
15th row K4, p4, k4, p2.
16th row K2, p4, C4F,
17th row As 16th row.
18th row C4FP, p2, k4, p4.
19th row K4, p4, k2, p2, k2.
20th row P2, C4FP, C4F, p4.
These 20 rows **form** patt panel A.

pattern B (worked over 14 sts)
1st to 10th rows As 11th to 20th rows of Patt A.
11th to 20th rows As 1st to 10th rows of Patt A.
These 20 rows **form** patt panel B.

to make
With 4mm (US 6) needles, cast on 102 sts.
1st row (right side) K2, [p2, k2] to end.
2nd row K2, p to last 2 sts, k2.
3rd (buttonhole) row K2, p2tog, yrn, k2, [p2, k2] to end.
4th row K2, p to last 2 sts, k2.
Rep 1st and 2nd rows once more.
Change to 4.50mm (US 7) needles.
Next row (right side) K2, p6, [k6, p8] twice, k6, p7, k2, turn and cont on these 51 sts only, leave rem 51 sts on a holder.
1st row (wrong side) K5, [work across 14 sts of 1st row of Patt A] 3 times, k4.

2nd row K2, p2, [work across 14 sts of 2nd row of Patt A] 3 times, p3, k2.
These 2 rows **set** the position of 3 patt panels with reverse st st and 2 sts in garter st at each end and are repeated 9 times more, working correct patt panel rows. When all 20 patt panel rows have been worked, rep 1st row once more.
Change to 4mm (US 6) needles.
Dec row (right side) K2, [p2, k2] 3 times, [p2tog, p1, k2, p1, p2tog, k2, p2, k2] twice, p2tog, p1, k2, p1, p2tog, k1. *45 sts.*
Leave these 45 sts on a holder.
With right side facing and 4.5mm (US 7) needles, rejoin yarn to 51 sts on first holder, k2, p7, [k6, p8] twice, k6, p6, k2.
1st row (wrong side) K4, [work across 14 sts of 1st row of Patt B] 3 times, k5.
2nd row K2, p3, [work across 14 sts of 2nd row of Patt B] 3 times, p2, k2.
These 2 rows **set** the position of 3 patt panels with reverse st st and 2 sts in garter st at each end and are repeated 9 times more, working correct patt panel rows. When all 20 patt panel rows have been worked, rep 1st row once more.
Change to 4mm (US 6) needles.
Dec row (right side) K1, p2tog, p1, k2, p1, p2tog, [k2, p2, k2, p2tog, p1, k2, p1, p2tog] twice, [k2, p2] 3 times, k2. *45 sts.*
Joining row (wrong side) K4, [p2, k2] to last 6 sts, p2, k4. *90 sts.*
Next row K2, [p2, k2] to end.
Next row K4, [p2, k2] to last 6 sts, p2, k4.
Rep the last 2 rows 3 times more.
Dec row (right side) K2, [k2tog] to last 2 sts, k2. *47 sts.*
Next row K2, p to last 2 sts, k2.
Buttonhole row K1, k2tog, yf, k to end.
Next row K2, p to last 2 sts, k2.
Next row K to end.
Rep the last 2 rows once more. Cast off knitwise.

to finish
Sew on buttons. Wrap around teapot and fasten buttons above and below handle.

Hot-Water Bottle Cover

When the weather has cooled and it's chilly both inside and out, a warming hot-water bottle is the ultimate comfort. Wrapped in a soft knitted cover, the plainest hot-water bottle is transformed into a thoughtful present. The simplicity of the textured ridge stitch is enhanced by this pastel pink, but you could plump for a neutral colour or even a brighter shade to complement an interior.

size
To fit a standard hot-water bottle from base to top of neck – 21 x 33cm (8¼ x 13in)

materials
✱ Two 50g balls of Debbie Bliss Cashmerino Aran in pale pink
✱ Pair of 4.50mm (US 7) knitting needles

tension
19 sts and 36 rows to 10cm (4in) square over patt using 4.50mm (US 7) needles.

abbreviations
See page 13.

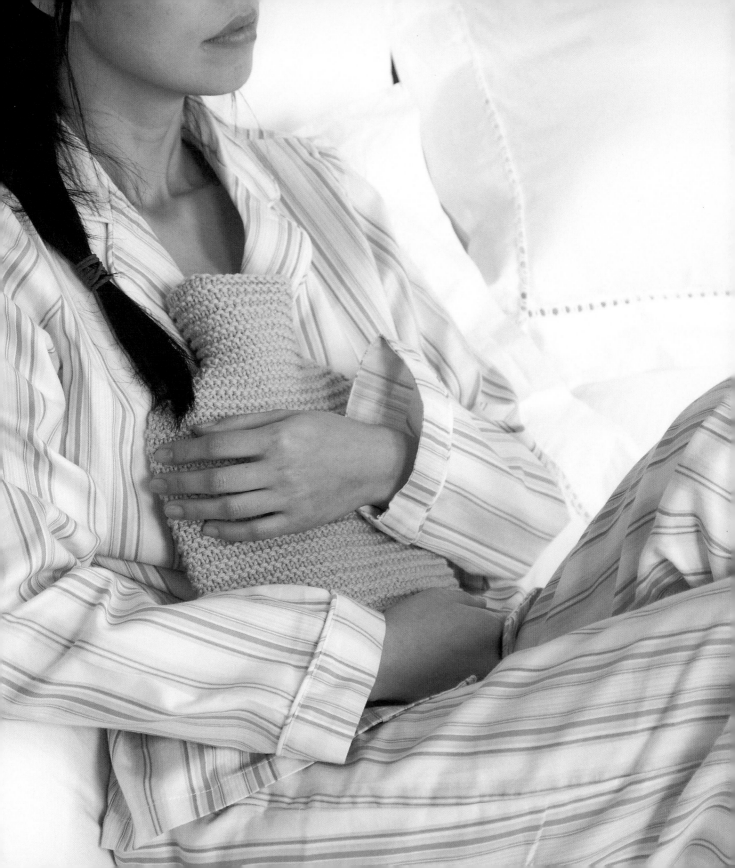

pattern

1st row (right side) K to end.
2nd row K to end.
3rd row K to end.
4th row P to end.
5th row P to end.
6th row P to end.
These 6 rows **form** the pattern and are repeated throughout.

to make

Worked in one piece from the base.
With 4.50mm (US 7) needles, cast on 75 sts.
Work in patt, as given above, until piece measures 23cm (9in) from cast on edge or until it reaches the start of the shoulder of your bottle, ending with a 2nd patt row.

Shape shoulders

1st row (right side) K17, skpo, k2tog, k33, skpo, k2tog, k17.
2nd row P16, p2tog tbl, p2tog, k31, p2tog tbl, p2tog, p16.
3rd row P15, p2tog tbl, p2tog, k29, p2tog tbl, p2tog, p15.
4th row P14, p2tog tbl, p2tog, k27, p2tog tbl, p2tog, p14.

5th row K13, skpo, k2tog, k25, skpo, k2tog, k13.
6th row K to end.
7th row K12, skpo, k2tog, k23, skpo, k2tog, k12.
8th row P to end.
9th row P11, p2tog tbl, p2tog, k21, p2tog tbl, p2tog, p11.
10th row P to end.
11th row K10, skpo, k2tog, k19, skpo, k2tog, k10.
12th row K to end.
13th row K9, skpo, k2tog, k17, skpo, k2tog, k9.
14th row P to end.
15th row P8, p2tog tbl, p2tog, k15, p2tog tbl, p2tog, p8.
35 sts.
Cont straight in patt for a further 15 rows, so ending with a 2nd patt row.
Cast off purlwise on right side, loosely but evenly.

to make up

Join the row ends to form the centre back seam, matching the ridge rows.
Join the base seam.
Insert the hot-water bottle into the finished cover before filling.

Moss Stitch Table Mats

Knitted in practical moss stitch in a robust washable cotton yarn, these mats offer a simple way to add colour to any table setting. When it comes to the colour pairings, literally anything goes. Make an entire set of these mats for all the members of your family, with a different colour combination for each person so everybody knows their place at the table.

size
Approximately 26 x 21cm (10¼ x 8in)

materials
4 mats
* 2 x 50g balls of Debbie Bliss Cotton DK in each of chocolate, stone, lime, pale green, teal, duck egg blue, fuchsia and red (see Note)
* Pair of 7mm (US 10½) knitting needles

tension
12 sts and 20 rows to 10cm (4in) square over moss st using the yarn double on 7mm (US 10½) needles.

abbreviations
See page 13.

note
Each mat is double sided and worked with 2 strands of yarn and you will need 2 balls of yarn for each side of each mat.

to make
Work one mat in each shade.
With 7mm (US 10½) needles and using the yarn double, cast on 25 sts.
Moss st row K1, [p1, k1] to end.
Rep this row until work measures 26cm (10¼in).
Cast off.

to finish
Pair up fuchsia with chocolate, stone with red, teal with pale green and lime with duck egg blue and join the pairs around the four sides.

Pot of Pansies

These knitted pansies are the ultimate hardy perennials. If you want to give a floral gift, but you know the recipient is not green fingered, these woolen flowers are the perfect choice. With no need to water, they provide an everlasting splash of cheery colour all year round.

size
Knitted cover to fit a 11cm (4¼in) flower pot

materials
* 1 x 50g ball of Debbie Bliss Rialto DK in rust, purple, green, gold and 1 x 50g ball of Debbie Bliss Riva in brown
* Pair each of 4mm (US 6), 5mm (US 8) and 7mm (US 10½) knitting needles
* Set of four 4mm (US 6) double-pointed knitting needles
* 11cm (4¼in) terracotta flower pot
* Oasis to fit pot or cut down to fit
* Florists wire
* Green plastic-coated wire
* Copydex glue or similar waterbased adhesive

tension
22 sts and 30 rows 10cm (4in) square over st st using 4mm (US 6) needles and Rialto DK for flower pot cover.

abbreviations
sk2togpo slip one knitwise, k2tog, pass slipped st over.
Also see page 13.

flowerpot

With 4mm (US 6) needles and rust, cast on 43 sts.
Beg with a k row, work 21 rows in st st, increasing 1 st at each end of 5th row and 4 foll 4th rows. *51 sts.*

Ridge row (wrong side) [With left hand needle, pick up loop of corresponding st 4 rows below and with right hand needle, p this st and next st on left hand needle tog] to end.

Change to 5mm (US 8) needles and beg with a k row, work 15 rows in st st.

Cut yarn and thread through sts on needle, do not pull up. Join the seam.

leaves

** With 4mm (US 6) double-pointed needles and green, cast on 3 sts and make a cord as follows:

1st row K3.

Next row Slide the sts to the opposite end of the needle without turning, pull the yarn tightly across the wrong side from left to right and k one row. **

Rep the last 2 rows until cord measures 2cm (¾in).
Now cont in rows as follows:

1st row (right side) K1, yf, k1, yf, k1. *5 sts.*
2nd row K2, p1, k2.
3rd row K2, yf, k1, yf, k2. *7 sts.*
4th row K3, p1, k3.
5th row K3, yf, k1, yf, k3. *9 sts.*
6th row K4, p1, k4.
7th row K4, yf, k1, yf, k4. *11 sts.*
8th row K5, p1, k5.
9th row K5, yf, k1, yf, k5. *13 sts.*
10th row K to end.
11th row Ssk, k to last 2 sts, k2tog.
Rep the last 2 rows 3 times more. *5 sts.*
18th row K to end.
19th row Ssk, k1, k2tog. *3 sts.*
20th row K to end.
21st row Sk2togpo.
Fasten off.

large petals (make 4)

With 4mm (US 6) needles and purple, cast on 8 sts.
Beg with a k row, work 4 rows in st st.
Cont in st st and inc 1 st at each end of next row and foll k row. *12 sts.*
P 1 row.
Cont in st st and dec 1 st at each end of next row and foll k row. *8 sts.*
P 1 row.
Cast off.

smaller petals (make 6)

With 4mm (US 6) needles and gold, cast on 8 sts.

Beg with a k row, work 4 rows in st st.

Cont in st st and inc 1 st at each end of next row. *10 sts.*

P 1 row.

Cont in st st and dec 1 st at each end of next row. *8 sts.*

P 1 row.

Cast off.

pansy stems (make 2)

With 4mm (US 6) needles and green, cast on 6 sts.

Beg with a k row, work 5cm (2in) in st st.

Cast off.

bud

With 4mm (US 6) needles and purple, cast on 4 sts.

Beg with a k row, work 10 rows in st st.

Change to gold and work 6 rows.

Cast off.

Roll the strip with the gold in the middle and sew the cast on edge down to form a tight tube.

bud leaf

Work as Leaves from ** to **.

Rep the last 2 rows until cord measures 5cm (2in).

Cont in rows as follows:

Next row K1, yf, k1, yf, k1. *5 sts.*

P 1 row.

Next row K1, [yf, k1] 4 times. *9 sts.*

P 1 row.

Next row K1, [yf, k1] 8 times. *17 sts.*

Next row Cast off 1, [slip st back onto left needle, cast on 2, cast off 5] to end.

Fasten off.

soil

With 7mm (US 10½) needles and brown and cast on 5 sts.

Next row K1, [p1, k1] to end.

This row **forms** the moss st and is repeated.

Working inc sts into moss st, inc one st at each end of next row and 5 foll alt rows. *17 sts.*

Moss st 2 rows.

Dec one st at each end of next row and 5 foll alt rows. *5 sts.*

Moss st one row.

Cast off.

to make up

petals

With right side facing and starting from centre of each cast off edge, thread florists wire around the outer edge of each petal, stretching the knitting slightly and leaving 6cm (2¼in) of wire free at each end. Oversew the edge with matching yarn.
Twist the two ends of wire together.

leaves

Thread green plastic-coated wire up through the stem, around the leaf and back down through the stem, leaving 8cm (3¼in) of wire free at each end. Twist the two ends of wire together.

bud

Wrap the bud leaf around the bud and secure. Thread green plastic-coated wire through stem and into the base of the bud and leaf, leaving around 8cm (3¼in) of wire free.

pansies

For the stem, cut a 10cm (4in) length of green plastic-coated wire, then arranging the petals as in picture to form a pansy 'face' with two large purple petals behind three gold petals, twist the petal wire around the stem wire. For each flower, wrap the pansy stem around the wires and join the row ends, leaving approx 8cm (3¼in) of wire free and sew stem to base of pansy, with seam at back. Using purple yarn, embroider a few long stitches onto the gold petals.

pot

Push the oasis into the pot, cutting to size if necessary and leaving approx 3cm (1¼in) space at the top. Place the pot cover over the pot, folding the excess over the top edge and glueing in place, also glue around the bottom edge of the pot to hold the cast on edge of the cover in place. Place the knitted soil on the top of the oasis, thread the stems of the leaves, the pansies and bud through the soil and push into the oasis as far as possible to hold in place, arranging them as in the photograph or as desired.

'Home Is Where The Heart Is' Cushion

This heart and home motif cushion makes the perfect housewarming gift to celebrate moving-in day. Worked in intarsia on stocking stitch, you could easily adjust the house shape to mirror the silhouette of the recipient's home. Or you could simply knit up the cushion incorporating just the heart motif as a special present for a loved one on Valentine's Day.

size
Approximately 41 x 41cm (16 x 16in)

materials
* 4 x 50g balls of Debbie Bliss Cashmerino Aran in ruby (A) and 1 x 50g ball in ecru (B)
* Pair of 5mm (US 8) knitting needles
* 41cm (16in) square cushion pad
* 3 buttons

tension
18 sts and 24 rows to 10cm (4in) square over st st using 5mm (US 8) needles.

abbreviations
y2rn yarn round needle twice to make 2 sts.
Also see page 13.

note
When working from chart, use separate small balls of yarn for each colour area and twist yarns at colour change to avoid holes.

to make

With 5mm (US 8) needles and A, cast on 77 sts.

Moss st row K1, [p1, k1] to end.

Rep this row 3 times more.

Beg with a k row, work 15 rows in st st, so ending with a k row.

Ridge row (wrong side) K to end.

Beg with a k row, cont in st st for a further 20 rows.

Next row K23, k across 31 sts of 1st row of chart, k23.

Next row P23, p across 31 sts of 2nd row of chart, p23.

These 2 rows **set** the position of the chart and are repeated.

Cont until all 61 rows have been worked.

Beg with a p row, cont in st st in A only for a further 20 rows, so ending with a k row.

Ridge row (wrong side) K to end.

Beg with a k row, work 88 rows in st st, so ending with a p row.

Buttonhole row [K16, skpo, y2rn, k2tog] 3 times, k17.

Next row P to end, working [p1, p1 tbl] into each y2rn.

Work 4 rows in moss st.

Cast off in moss st.

to make up

Fold cover along ridge rows and join side seams from fold to cast on edge, then join side seams from fold to cast off edge, working through all thicknesses where cover overlaps. Sew on buttons. Insert cushion pad and fasten buttons.

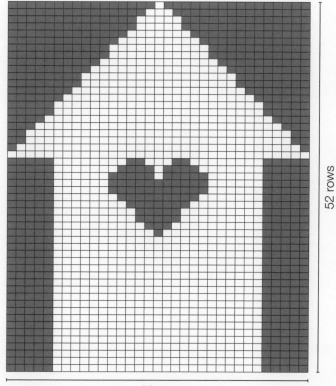

52 rows

33 sts

Key

■ A

□ B

Striped Pencil Pot Cover

I love the colourful organisation that these pots bring to my work desk at home, however, these super-simple striped covers needn't be just for pencils. The pattern can easily be adjusted to suit any size container, so you can tailor them to fit any vessel; why not team the stripes with a friend's favourite colour blooms to make a cover for a flower vase or even a tall jar to house knitting needles.

size
To fit a 10cm (4in) high straight-sided container (see end of instructions for other sizes)

materials
✳ Oddments of Debbie Bliss Rialto DK in each of four colours (A, B, C, and D – see Note).
✳ Pair of 3.75mm (US 5) knitting needles

tension
24 sts and 42 rows to 10cm (4in) square over garter st using 3.75mm (US 5) needles.

note
We used approximately 8g in each of navy (A), lime (B), burnt orange (C) and teal (D).

abbreviations
See page 13.

to make
With 3.75mm (US 5) needles and D, cast on 24 sts using the two needle cable method.
1st row (wrong side) K to end.
Working in garter st (k every row), cont in 2 row stripes of A, B, C and D until the strip, when very slightly stretched, fits around the container, ending, where possible, with a two row stripe in A.
Cast off in D.
Join the cast on and cast off edges together.

to resize the cover
Measure the height of your container, then using the tension of 24 sts to 10cm (4in) (2.4 sts to 1cm or 6 sts to 1in), calculate the number of sts you will need to cast on. For example: if you are using a container which is 11cm high, multiply 11 x 2.4 = 26.4 sts, so you would cast on 27 sts.

For suppliers of Debbie Bliss yarns
please contact:

UK & WORLDWIDE DISTRIBUTORS
Designer Yarns Ltd
Units 8–10
Newbridge Industrial Estate
Pitt Street
Keighley
West Yorkshire BD21 4PQ
UK
t: +44 (0) 1535 664222
e: enquiries@designeryarns.uk.com
w: www.designeryarns.uk.com

USA
Knitting Fever Inc.
315 Bayview Avenue
Amityville
NY 11701
USA
t: +1 (516) 546 3600
w: www.knittingfever.com

CANADA
Diamond Yarns Ltd.
155 Martin Ross Avenue
Unit 3
Toronto
Ontario M3J 2L9
Canada
t: +1 (416) 736 6111
w: www.diamondyarn.com

MEXICO
Estambres Crochet SA de CV
Aaron Saenz 1891–7
Col. Santa Maria
Monterrey
N.L. 64650
Mexico
t: +52 (81) 8335 3870
e: abremer@redmundial.com.mx

DENMARK
Fancy Knit
Hovedvejen 71, 8586 Oerum Djurs
Ramten
Denmark
t: +45 59 46 21 89
e: roenneburg@mail.dk

FINLAND
Eiran Tukku
Mäkelänkatu 54 B
00510 Helsinki
Finland
t: +358 50 346 0575
e: maria.hellbom@eirantukku.fi
w: www.eirantukku.fi

FRANCE
Plassard Diffusion
La Filature
71800 Varennes-sous-Dun
France
t: +33 (0) 3 8528 2828
e: info@laines-plassard.com

GERMANY/AUSTRIA/ SWITZERLAND/ BENELUX
Designer Yarns (Deutschland) GmbH
Welserstraße 10g
D-51149 Köln
Germany
t: +49 (0) 2203 1021910
e: info@designeryarns.de
w: www.designeryarns.de

ICELAND
Storkurinn ehf
Laugavegi 59
101 Reykjavík
Iceland
t: +354 551 8258
e: storkurinn@simnet.is

SPAIN
Oyambre Needlework SL
Balmes, 200 At. 4
08006 Barcelona
Spain
t: +34 (0) 93 487 26 72
e: info@oyambreonline.com

SWEDEN
Nysta garn och textil
Hogasvagen 20
S-131 47 Nacka
Sweden
t: +46 708 81 39 54
e: info@nysta.se
w: www.nysta.se

RUSSIA
Golden Fleece Ltd
Soloviyny proezd 16
117593 Moscow
Russia
t: +8 (903) 000 1967
e: natalya@rukodelie.ru
w: www.rukodelie.ru

NORWAY
Viking of Norway
Bygdaveien 63
4333 Oltedal
Norway
e: post@viking-garn.no
w: www.viking-garn.no

CHINA
Lotus Textile Co Ltd.
77 Zhonghua W. St.
Xingtai
Hebei, 05-4000
China
e: hanpsheng@yahoo.com.cn

AUSTRALIA/NEW ZEALAND

Prestige Yarns Pty Ltd.
P.O. Box 39, Bulli
NSW 2516
Australia
t: +61 (0) 2 4285 6669
e: info@prestigeyarns.com
w: www.prestigeyarns.com

HONG KONG

East Unity Company Ltd
Unit B2
7/F Block B
Kailey Industrial Centre
12 Fung Yip Street
Chan Wan
t: (852) 2869 7110
e: eastunity@yahoo.com.hk

TAIWAN

U-Knit
1F, 199-1 Sec
Zhong Xiao East Road
Taipei
Taiwan
t: +886 2 27527557
e: shuindigo@hotmail.com

THAILAND

Needle World Co Ltd
Pradit Manoontham Road
Bangkok 10310
Thailand
t: +662 933 9167
e: needle-world.coltd@googlemail.com

BRAZIL

Quatro Estacoes Com
Las Linhas e Acessorios Ltda
Av. Das Nacoes Unidas
12551-9 Andar
Cep 04578-000 Sao Paulo
Brazil
t: +55 11 3443 7736
e: cristina@4estacoeslas.com.br

For more information on my other
books and yarns, please visit
www.debbieblissonline.com

Acknowledgements

This book would not have been possible without the generous collaboration of the following people: Rosy Tucker, who played a huge part in producing projects and working on ideas for this book. Jane O'Shea and Lisa Pendreigh at Quadrille Publishing who are wonderful to work with and make each book I publish with them a joy. Katherine Case for the fantastic book design. Mia Pejcinovic, the stylist, for capturing the idea and the look of the book perfectly. Penny Wincer for the beautiful photography and baby Arthur for his exquisite toes in the baby blanket. Penny Hill for essential pattern compiling and organising knitters. The knitters for creating perfect knits under deadline pressure: Mrs Baker, Cynthia Brent, Pat Church, Shirley Kenneth, Maisie Lawrence, Mrs Reay, Frances Wallace and Mrs Watson. Heather Jeeves, a fantastic agent. The distributors, agents, retailers and knitters who support all my books and yarns with enthusiasm and make everything I do possible.

Editorial Director Jane O'Shea
Creative Director Helen Lewis
Project Editor Lisa Pendreigh
Designer Katherine Case
Photographer Penny Wincer
Stylist Mia Pejcinovic
Production Director Vincent Smith
Production Controller Leonie Kellman

First published in 2011 by
Quadrille Publishing Limited
Alhambra House
27–31 Charing Cross Road
London WC2H 0LS
www.quadrille.co.uk

Text and project designs © 2011
Debbie Bliss
Photography, design and layout © 2011
Quadrille Publishing Ltd

The rights of Debbie Bliss to be identified as the author of this work have been asserted by her in accordance with the Copyright, Design, and Patents Act 1988.

British Library Cataloguing-in-Publication Data
A catalogue record for this book is available from the British Library.

ISBN 978 184400 977 0

Printed in China